T·H·E
VICTORIOUS
CHRISTIAN
LIFE

DR. TONY EVANS

A
JANET
THOMA
BOOK

THOMAS NELSON PUBLISHERS
Nashville

Published in Nashville, Tennessee, by Janet Thoma Books, a division of Thomas Nelson, Inc., Publishers, and distributed in Canada by Word Communications, Ltd., Richmond, British Columbia, and in the United Kingdom by Word (UK), Ltd., Milton Keynes, England.

ISBN 0–8407–3448–4

Printed in the United States of America

CONTENTS

CONTENTS

PART ONE

VICTORY— PLAYING TO WIN

1

THE THRILL OF VICTORY, THE AGONY OF DEFEAT

JANUARY 31, 1993, was a bittersweet day in America, depending on where you lived. That was the day the Dallas Cowboys dismantled the Buffalo Bills in Superbowl XXVII. If you lived in Dallas, you celebrated the thrill of victory. If you lived in Buffalo, you suffered the agony of defeat. In Dallas there were parties, victory parades, and celebration upon celebration. In Buffalo there was guilt (team members thinking, *We really didn't play as well as we could have*), discouragement, and complaints. While both teams took the field, only one was victorious.

Unfortunately what was true of Superbowl XXVII is also true of the Christian life. While all Christians navigate the Christian terrain through faith in Christ, not all are victorious. Some Christians win the battle; they rejoice in their relationship with Christ. And even though that means getting bumped and bruised along the way, they still are able to score touchdowns for God. Conversely, others—who are equally bumped and bruised—fumble regularly (like the Buffalo Bills!), and as soon as they are ready to mount some forward momentum, the other side gains the upper hand and forces them to punt or throw an interception. While they muster a big play or two from time to time, the spiritual momentum necessary to sustain a lifelong drive of holiness and spiritual victory is just not there. In spite of the fact that they go to their weekly huddles—the church—and in spite of the fact that they know all the plays of Scripture, a blitz by the opposition throws them for a loss.

Many people discover that life is like a touchdown scored after the whistle has blown. As soon as it seems they have achieved victory in life, they discover it doesn't count. Maybe you have felt that way—life is all pushing for yardage but never making a firstdown, reaching for the long pass and then having it intercepted.

This cry is heard in the complaint of a single mother trapped by poverty, not knowing where to find the father of her child. This cry is heard in the frustration of a black man who has not been able to rise from the level of "boy" in the eyes of his employer and, thus, cannot adequately support his family. This cry is heard in the behavior of a teenage mother who, realizing that she has missed out on the "fun" years of her adolescence, abuses her child or neglects him while she tries to catch up with her single friends.

The well-to-do in our society camouflage their misery a little better and a little longer than those who live at the lower end of the ladder of success, but their cry is just the same. Some look for meaning in a career while others look for it in relationships. Some drink for it; others snort for it. Some—the most miserable—give up and make the ultimate exit in suicide because they can't find any meaning.

That's how Satan wants us to feel. He is overjoyed when we feel confused, frustrated, and defeated, because he doesn't want us to find meaning and value in life. He works hard to set up cardboard imitations of life (dishonest or immoral lifestyles for some, alcohol or drugs for others) and is delighted when people are fooled into believing they are true. These stage props trip us and make the going harder and harder.

And if Satan can't take us out with ungodly lifestyles, he'll try another method. Satan is crafty. He's not the funny man with horns depicted in cartoons. Christ knew his true nature and called him a murderer and the father of lies (see John 8:44). Satan is the accuser of the righteous (see Rev. 12:10), and his business is to destroy believers through every technique imaginable. If money will lead a believer astray, he'll give him power. If a new job with a more attractive salary will move God's child away from the Father's will, Satan will help him get the job.

God has provided us with the armor to withstand any attack, but Satan will try every trick to find the chink in a Christian's armor. And no matter what his method, his goal is simple: to keep the believer from experiencing the victorious Christian life.

THE PATH TO DEFEAT

The Bible contains one whole book dedicated to exploring the meaning of life. God knew we would question our meaning, so He was careful in choosing the author of it. He knew He had to choose someone who would have instant and lasting respectability. King Solomon was His choice, and Ecclesiastes is the name of the book.

If any man should have had a full and meaningful life, it was Solomon. Yet the opening words of Ecclesiastes are, "'Vanity of vanities, all is vanity.'" Quite a downer for a book about life!

When I served as a professor of homiletics at Dallas Theological Seminary, I would tell the young men in my Basics of Preaching class to start their sermons with a compelling introduction that would capture the interest of their audiences so they would want to hear more. Surprisingly, Solomon used a technique contrary to that proven principle. He told the reader right up front that he had nothing to say because life was all emptiness and vanity.

Solomon wrote the Book of Ecclesiastes toward the end of his life, as he was looking back, asking the typical questions about its meaning: Who am I? Why am I here? Where am I going?

In spite of a life of great prestige, responsibility, and luxury, he gave the same answer to these questions as the single mother trapped by poverty—much of life is empty. If King Solomon could say life is meaningless, what about the rest of us? Can an unemployed steel worker find meaning and victory in life when he can't support his family? Can a sick, elderly woman trying to support herself on a small fixed income experience fullness? Can a successful, two-income couple avoid the ruts that scar the track of the rat race?

Solomon's opening words suggest a negative answer to all of those questions, but let's not stop reading too soon. In spite of this ominous beginning, Solomon did have a positive message for each of us, no matter what our age or lifestyle.

This king tried all the lifestyles—as only the richest man in the world could—and evaluated three of the major ones: pleasure, knowledge, and work. Solomon took the pleasure route first, thinking that if he had enough fun and good times, he'd have a reason for living.

Can Meaning Be Found in Pleasure?

Chapter 2 describes Solomon's plan to fill his life with all the pleasure possible. He admitted, "I searched in my heart how to gratify my flesh with wine" (v. 3).

Solomon would have been right at home in the 1990s. The only difference is, he experimented with alcohol, whereas today we have added mind-altering uppers and downers, pills, powders, and crystals to the list of substances available for abuse. Like today's joy-seekers, Solomon was looking for thrills. That's the case with too many people whose lives have holes in them as big as Mack trucks, and they're looking for something with which to fill them. These people are desperately trying to find solutions to the problem of meaninglessness, but their solutions only lead to bigger problems. And these aren't just people who've lived long enough to experience deep discouragement and defeat. According to the National Council on Alcoholism, an estimated 4.6 million adolescents between the ages of fourteen and seventeen experienced the negative consequences of alcohol abuse in 1985. Terrible statistics—but nothing new. In fact, Solomon said there is nothing new under the sun.

So Solomon turned to another source of pleasure— material possessions.

If Not Thrills, Then Material Possessions

You may know what it is like to look forward eagerly to something special, and then find when you finally experience it there is no joy in it. You may have looked forward to buying a new car, then when you bought it—whoosh—the excitement was gone. You may have looked and looked for that special new house, but soon after you bought it, it became just a place to hang your hat. Even your mate may not be as exciting as you remember him or her when you met. Things tend to get boring quickly. Solomon learned the truth of that experience. He said in Ecclesiastes 2:4–6, "I made my works great, I built myself houses, and planted myself vineyards. I made myself gardens and orchards, and I planted all kinds of fruit trees in them. I made myself water pools from which to water the growing trees of the grove."

(There's a key word in these verses. Have you caught it?) "I acquired male and female servants, and had servants born in my house. Yes, I had greater possessions of herds and flocks that all who were in Jerusalem before me. I also gathered myself silver and gold and the special treasures of kings and of the provinces. I acquired male and femlae singers, the delights of the sons of men, and musical instruments of all kinds" (vv. 2:7, 8). (Have you picked out that key word yet? It's the word *I*.)

Verse 10 sums up Solomon's activities: "Whatever my eyes desired I did not keep from them." Solomon didn't go to the party; he brought the party to himself. But there was one problem. When the party was over, after all that frenzied activity, he realized that it was all vanity and striving after wind. Have you ever tried to catch the wind? It's an exercise in futility. Every time you grab, it slips through your fingers.

Solomon rejected pleasure as an answer to his meaninglessness. Instead he turned to a pursuit of knowledge.

Can Meaning Be Found Through Knowledge?

Since the answers Solomon was seeking weren't to be found in pleasure and material possessions, he tried another angle: education. He told himself, *"The wise man's eyes are in his head, but the fool walks in darkness"* (2:14). Solomon was saying, "It's better to be smart than ignorant" (which is not all that different from the parents today who tell their children, "You must get a college education"). So Solomon set out to become well-educated. And he accomplished exactly that; the Bible says he became the wisest man on earth.

Not only did he have a vast amount of knowledge, but he also possessed a unique ability to appropriately apply that knowledge to the human situation, which is the true nature of biblical wisdom.

Did his education or its application give him a reason for living? No. In fact, it probably made him even more miserable. He realized that his fate was no better than that of the biggest fool in town since most of the misfortunes that could happen to a fool (the death of a loved one, his own illness, his own death) could as easily happen to him. Since his Ph.D. in world knowledge was no protection, he decided that education, too, was emptiness.

Perhaps I should add a disclaimer here. Even though one cannot find the true meaning of life in education, educated citizens are still essential to make our democratic form of government function well. Also a person will probably not be able to find a satisfying job without at least a high school education within our democratic/capitalistic system (although many people are finding a college degree no longer guarantees a good job).

I ask myself how my ancestors who were in slavery could have had so much common sense with so little formal training, whereas many of their grandchildren and great-grandchildren have B.A.s, M.A.s, and Ph.D.s, and yet still do not know who they are, why they are here, or where they are going. Solomon was right. Education can improve the quality of life, but, ultimately, it can't make life worth living.

Neither pleasure nor knowledge gave life meaning, but Solomon wasn't ready to give up his search so easily. Next, he decided that work might fill the void in his life, give him a reason to get up in the morning, keep him occupied, challenged, and enthusiastic about living. So he turned his attention to his job.

Can Meaning Be Found through Work?

No one could possibly have had a better position than Solomon, the king of the great nation of Israel. People came from all over the world to meet and talk with him. His work must have given great purpose to his life. But did it? Verses 18 and 19 of chapter 2 say, "I hated my labor in which I had toiled under the sun, because I must leave it to the man who will come after me. And who knows whether he will be a wise man or a fool? Yet he will rule over all my labor in which I toiled and in which I have shown myself wise under the sun."

Solomon was saying, "I am breaking my neck to build up Israel, and when I die somebody is going to take my place. I don't know if he'll be someone I'd approve of or if I would agree with the way he'll do things, but he is going to take my place and, worse yet, get for free what it took me a lifetime to build."

I've had glimpses of Solomon's disillusionment. I fly approximately fifty thousand miles a year on speaking engagements. If the plane were to crash and I were to die, my wife would certainly grieve for a while. But being young and beautiful, she would probably remarry. That's OK. I wouldn't want her to live her life alone. But still that thought bothers me a little. The man she would marry might move into *my* house—for which he would not have paid one dime. He might drive *my* car and maybe even wear some of *my* clothes. He would receive those things for free because I would not be around anymore. That's a bitter thought to chew on if work gives life meaning.

Solomon felt this irony even more because he ruled a whole nation. That is what led him to write lines that have become famous: "To everything there is a season. . . . A time to be born, and a time to die; a time to plant, and a time to pluck what is planted . . . A time of war, and a time of peace" (Ecc. 3:1, 2, 8).

He said, you and I can make contributions, but we work within a system that is already planned, functioning, and unchangeable. We are locked in by death as well as by life, by misery as well as by happiness. Solomon concluded, "Why work if God's got us pinned in this way?" (see 3:9).

So Solomon discarded work and looked for yet another answer to his questions, Who am I? Why am I here? Where am I going?

THE ROAD TO VICTORY

Solomon finally saw God's plan for his life in Ecclesiastes 3:11: "He has made everything beautiful in its time. Also, he has put eternity in their hearts."

There's the answer to Solomon's search for meaning in life: God has set eternity into the hearts of mankind. Knowing that gives purpose to life.

The phrase "eternity in their hearts" means God has placed a big question mark deep in every man's soul. We *should* be asking the question, What is the meaning of life? God intended it that way. But there is nothing in finite time that can provide the answer to that cosmic question.

Many of us have lost sight of the fact that life and its labor are from God. We believe we've earned those things. We get up in the morning and say, "Here's my agenda. I'm going to do this, this, and this."

Then we get irritated, aggravated, and even angry when things interrupt those plans. We've forgotten that our lives are not our own. They are God's, and it is His work we are here to do. The plans, the timing, and the assignment are all His.

For this reason the apostle James warned businessmen against setting their own agendas. He reminded them that their lives were nothing more than a "vapor," which would vanish in a short time, and exhorted them to plan in a new way (see James 4:14). "Come now, you who say, 'Today or tomorrow we will go to such and such a city, spend a year there, buy and sell, and make a profit,' " James said, instead you should plan by saying, " 'If the Lord wills, we shall live and also do this or that' " (v. 13, 15).

Do you want purpose in life? Do you want meaning in place of emptiness? Do you want victory instead of defeat? Then prioritize God. Without God as our priority, our lives will wind up being just like the one Solomon described in Ecclesiastes—full of vanity and emptiness. Pleasure, education, the job, designer clothing, an expensive sports car, crowds or friends— these can never give life meaning. They are fillers, not substance.

Jesus said, "Unless a grain of wheat falls into the ground and dies, it remains alone; but if it dies, it produces much grain" (John 12:24). Only when you die to self—that is, forget yourself and start living for Him—will you find the abundant life.

We all choose each day between the agony of defeat and the thrill of victory.

The concept of this book was born from my experience as a pastor. I have witnessed many Christians who move from one problem to another, perpetually living in the agony of defeat. As a Christian, I too have had to deal with lost spiritual yardage. On the other hand I have also observed Christians who face the same headaches and heartaches, joys and sorrows, of the defeated Christian, only they somehow find ways to make the opposition fumble and come up with big plays necessary to be winners. What is the difference between the two?

Those who are victorious don't let the opposition throw them off their game plan. They prepare hard by studying the enemy and focusing intensely on executing God's plan even in the midst of conflict. Defeated Christians, however, allow the circumstances to redefine their strategy. The opposition beats them mercilessly until they are just too weak to fight back.

Any expert on the game of football rarely ignores the statistics of time of possession and team turnovers. The team that keeps the ball the longest usually wins the game, and the team with the most turnovers usually loses the game. The same thing is true of our spiritual lives. If we are to be victorious, then we must keep Satan on the defensive and cease turning over our lives to him. If we are to experientially know what it means to be more than conquerors in Christ, then we will need to seriously accept our responsibility to remain faithful to the play book of God, the Bible, and courageously prevent the enemy's plot from governing our lives.

I hope this book will enable defeated Christians to reverse their negative momentum through consistent and progressive spiritual firstdowns. No matter how lopsided the score, if you can mount a proper defense and keep scoring yourself, you can change the outcome. This book is also designed to encourage victorious Christians to maintain their advantage, for our adversary is looking for any and every opportunity to reverse the positive momentum (and ultimately the outcome of our lives).

In Part One we will look at who we are in Christ, once we have joined His team. In Part Two we will look at the process of spiritual growth, which is as old as Peter's and Paul's advice to the early Christians and as new as yours and my own experience. The pieces of this process—Scripture, prayer, the local church, and the grace of giving—are necessary for surviving the skirmishes and losses of life. We'll look at some of those difficulties in Part Three, "Overcoming the Opposing Team." Finally, we will get a glimpse of the thrill of victory—our welcome into God's eternal kingdom.

Many of the suggestions for how to live a victorious Christian life aren't mine. They come from a few of my mentors: the apostle Paul and other apostles who helped the early Christians grow into spiritual maturity. Those first Christians may have worn long robes rather than mini-skirts and shorts, and tended sheep rather than computers, but their thoughts and feelings and problems and sins were very similar to ours. Throughout this book we will look at the apostles' advice to these wayward saints in the letters they wrote to early churches in Corinth, Rome, Philippi, and Jerusalem.

God has saved us to be victorious and we should be satisfied with nothing less than knowing that we are experiencing, day by day, the spiritual reality of John's words, "Greater is He that is in us than he that is in the world." It's time to move forward to enjoy the thrill of victory.

2

A MILLION-DOLLAR CONTRACT: THE MAGNIFICENT GRACE OF GOD

ONE OF THE most popular TV programs of the late 1950s was a show called "The Millionaire," in which a nameless, faceless multimillionaire found great joy in dispensing one million dollars each week to some unsuspecting soul.

I'm sure the reason the show was so popular was that everyone watching it wanted to receive so gracious a gift. The mysterious benefactor, who was only revealed by his voice and sometimes the back of his head, would authorize his agent, Michael Anthony, to dispense the million dollar check to the person who had been selected that week. Some of the people were poor, others were middle class, and a few were relatively wealthy already.

How would the recipient respond to the gift? we all wondered. Some people rejected it all together, refusing to believe that anyone could possibly be so kind and generous. They simply continued life as usual, never benefitting from the benefactor's wealth. Others rejected it at first, but after Michael Anthony convinced them, their disbelief turned into great joy.

The rest of the show was devoted to answering the next obvious question: How will they spend their money? Some squandered the funds quickly; others invested them wisely. Some selfishly hoarded the money for themselves; some shared the gift with others. Some became dissatisfied with the amount (after all, two million would be even better), while others rejoiced at so liberal a gift. Whatever the response, each weekly episode was filled with drama and excitement, laughter and tears, as Michael Anthony encountered a variety of situations and sometimes dangerous circumstances. At the end of each show Anthony would report back to the benefactor, telling him if the gift had been accepted. Regardless of the recipient's response, the multimillionaire was always willing to give again.

I find this a most accurate and appropriate illustration of the magnificent grace of God. Our wealthy, eternal Benefactor, who is transcendent (thus distinct from His creation), sent His only Son, Jesus Christ, to bestow His spiritual wealth upon you and me—sinful, undeserving men and women. And we respond to God's generous provision in a variety of ways. Some of us reject God's gift outright, while others reject it initially, then change their minds. Some cry when they accept it, others laugh. Some change their lifestyles quickly, while others change much more gradually.

Some express overwhelming gratitude to the eternal Benefactor's generosity by praising His Representative, Jesus Christ, while others receive Him with little thankfulness. Some who receive God's gift later squander it and have little to show for the provisions of God's grace. However, one thing is true of all of these people. They have been provided a generous opportunity to become spiritual millionaires.

THE MAGNIFICENT GRACE OF GOD

Recently, while window shopping (my favorite kind of shopping) in a local mall with my wife, we ventured into a jewelry store to look at the various diamonds on display. We came across one particularly large and beautiful stone that was irresistibly attractive. We asked if we could look more closely at it, so the proprietor unlocked the case and lifted out the diamond. Before showing it, however, he took out a black velvet cloth and placed the diamond in the center. Something amazing happened when the stone was placed against the backdrop of the dark cloth. Its brilliance was enhanced to an almost blinding degree.

This is like the grace of God. By itself, it shines brightly. His goodness wakes us up each morning, provides oxygen for us to breathe, rain and sunshine so our crops can grow, and natural resources so we can live comfortably on this planet. Theologians call this "common grace," which is available to all men everywhere. However, when this common grace is placed against the black backdrop of man's sin, God's grace blinds us with its brilliance.

The grace of God is best expressed as "getting God's absolute best when we deserve the absolute worst."

Theologians frequently refer to God's grace as "un-merited favor." The New Testament word for *grace*, the word *charis*, carries the idea of "favor," "gratitude," or "goodwill." Christ brought us exceedingly abundant blessings, despite the fact that we did not deserve them.

Well, actually, we did deserve something: divine judgment. We were destitute, having no hope whatsoever. As sinners, our future was bright—not due to the glory of God, but to the fires of hell. God had the free choice of placing us in hell because of our sinfulness. Moreover, He could have even charged us rent for being there!

Before Christ, we lived in a graveyard called "trespasses and sins," corpses unable to do anything to satisfy the demands of a Holy God (Rom. 3:23). The coroner's report from God declares that all mankind exists in a spiritual mortuary, and while there may be varying degrees of decomposition—some are sick and dead, others poor and dead, some white and dead, others black and dead—all are equally dead, totally without the life of God within them.

A hundred years ago when a person died, he would be buried rather crudely. The deceased would be placed in a wooden coffin, broad at the top and narrow at the bottom. He would be transported to the closest cemetery in a horse-drawn carriage and lowered into the ground by a rope, which was wrapped around the top and bottom of the box.

However, today when you die, you die in style. You are placed in a rather expensive bronze casket, which is lined with linen. You get to rest your head on a satin pillow. You are dressed by professionals who manicure your nails, comb your hair, and fix your clothes (matter of fact, I've seen some people who looked better dead than they ever looked alive!). As you leave the church for the burial grounds, you ride in a limousine, a lifelong dream for some of us. In fact, a fleet of limousines lead by two men on motorcycles who stop traffic as you ride through red lights on your way to your final resting place. Finally, you are lowered into the ground by a smooth, nickel-plated machine.

The bottom line, however, is still the same: Dead is dead. And that's God's verdict on all of humanity outside of Christ. The unregenerate are walking zombies entombed by this world order, the control of the devil, and the desires of their own flesh They deserve God's wrath, not His grace. Not a very pretty picture but a necessary one if grace is to ever make sense.

Yet while we were weak, while we were dead in our trespasses and sins, God being rich in mercy, demonstrated His own love toward us. He did not spare His one-of-a-kind Son. He reconciled us to Himself. Then He made us alive with Him and seated us with Him in heavenly places.

Now that's a mouthful, and yet, it does not even come close to all that the Bible declares about the grace of God. We owe both our existence and our state of being to God and His marvelous plan of redemption. (In fact, we did not even know that we were in need of salvation until God told us! God's grace rescued us from the eternal and hideous consequences of sin, while we were yet ignorant of our impending tragedy.) Therefore, all boasting should be about the Lord and not about ourselves.

It's like the story told of an Indian who had become a Christian. As his brothers began to observe how different his lifestyle had become, they asked, "What has caused such a change?" The new Christian looked on the ground and found a worm; then he put it on some leaves and set them aflame. Just before the fire got to the worm, he reached down and took the worm out of the flames and held it before his friends. "Me—worm," he said.

That is what God did for each of us. He reached down to sinful men, who deserved the fire of judgment, and just in the nick of time, delivered us up from the flames so we might live a life pleasing to Him. The apostle Paul told it all: "But God, who is rich in mercy, because of His great love with which He loved us, even when were dead in trespasses, made us alive together with Christ (by grace you have been saved), and raised us up together, and made us sit together in the heavenly places in Christ Jesus, that in the ages to come He might show the exceeding riches of His grace in His kindness toward us in Christ Jesus" (Eph. 2:4–7).

THE SUFFICIENCY OF CHRIST

We must understand that if we depend upon anything beyond Jesus for salvation, then we're really saying, "Jesus Christ alone is not enough."

The whole point of the Gospel is:

> Jesus Christ plus **nothing** equals salvation.
> Jesus plus **anything** equals damnation.

After all, if God Himself could not get the job done on the cross, what other force in the universe could possibly hope to make any difference?

If I died right now and God asked me why He should admit me to heaven, I wouldn't bring up the fact that I was a preacher. I wouldn't point out that I had been faithful to my wife. I wouldn't mention that I did the best I could to live a good life. I wouldn't refer to my twelve years of theological training, or to my generosity, my compassion, my charitable ventures. All would be equally irrelevant.

As I faced God, I'd call out to Jesus. "Jesus, there's a list of sins in that book right there. And I'm guilty on every count. But when I was eleven years old, I got down on my knees and told you that I was a sinner. I told you I believe that when you died on that cross, you died for me. I believe that you have already paid my penalty. And Jesus, you are all I have!" Nothing I can add, no contribution I might make, no service I can render would help my case on Judgment Day. The only question on the floor then is, "What have you done with Jesus Christ?"

God is waiting for you to commit the entire weight of your existence to Jesus Christ and what He did on the cross.

You might say, "But my mama was a Christian. And she prayed for me!" Praise God! Your mama is in heaven. Now, what about you? Christianity has nothing to do with your heritage, it has nothing to do with the name of the church you attend. It has to do with whether or not you have placed absolute confidence in the person and work of Christ.

In 1929, a man named George Wilson robbed the U.S. Mail and, in the act, committed a murder. He was later arrested, tried, convicted, and sentenced to be hanged. Some of his friends petitioned President Andrew Jackson for a pardon. Though that pardon was granted, Wilson refused to accept it! Well, this was a one-of-a-kind situation. Eventually, the matter came before the U.S. Supreme Court. In their decision,

Justice Marshall explained that in order to be valid, a pardon must be accepted by the condemned person. While it is virtually inconceivable that a person sentenced to death would refuse a pardon, that person had the right to do so. George Wilson was executed while his written pardon lay on the sheriff's desk.

Many people will not make it to God's heaven, even though Jesus has already affixed His signature on their pardon, because they will personally receive it.

All of this is by grace, "For by grace you have been saved through faith, and that not of yourselves; it is the gift of God, not of works, lest anyone should boast" (Eph. 2:8–9). Our salvation is not based on who we are or what we have done but on who God is and what He has done. In fact, any and all attempts to merit God's grace (for example, by works) are futile and nullify the very salvation we seek to attain.

This picture of grace apart from works was graphically revealed to me some years ago when I was serving as a water safety instructor for the YMCA. A rather large man was drowning in the middle of the pool. I dove in to save him, but in his fight to save himself, he was negating my ability to rescue him. His attempts at self-deliverance, while sincere, were only grabbing chunks of air. I simply treaded water while I waited for him to stop trying.

I could tell by the way he looked at me that it horrified him to see me so close and yet so far. Yet there was a stark reality, *I could not be his savior if he insisted on saving himself.* Finally, he gave up. He was just too water-logged to save himself. That's when I took over. I swam behind him, placed his head in my hand, and pulled him to the pool deck. When he came to himself, he looked at me and exclaimed, "Thank you for saving me!"

Another incident like this did not end so pleasantly. A 250-pound high-school sophomore, who was a star football player, dove from a pontoon boat into Lake Wylie in South Carolina to retrieve a beach ball. The unanchored boat drifted away from him and as an inexperienced swimmer he panicked. A friend tried to save him, but was pulled down by the young man's violent efforts to save himself. That football player never gave up. Instead he drowned in the 34-foot deep waters.

Grace only saves you when you cease trying to save yourself and entrust yourself to Jesus Christ and His finished work on the cross for your sins. Grace pulls you to the shore so that your life can begin again.

Before we explore the subject of the victorious Christian life any further, you must be assured of your spiritual birth. Have you ever taken this vital step? Have you confessed your sinfulness to Jesus Christ and trusted Him alone for your salvation? If not, there's no better time than right now.

It all begins with a simple prayer of faith. The exact wording isn't important—what matters is your sincerity. Here's an example:

> Lord Jesus, I confess that I am a sinner. I have failed to reflect Your glory and deserve the punishment that results from sin. But Jesus, I don't want to die; I want to live in heaven with You. I believe that You are holy and sinless, that You died on the cross at Calvary in my place and rose from the dead to secure my salvation. I now place all my confidence in You to be my Savior. Please forgive my sin and give me new life. Thank You for saving me. I want to live my life for You. Amen.

If you prayed that prayer for the first time, don't keep it a secret. Talk with your pastor or a Christian friend. Let them know about your decision so they can encourage you and help you to grow in your newfound faith. Find a church that teaches the Bible and get involved right away. New Christians need this kind of care and attention.

Once you accept this gift of grace, you are ready to forge ahead and discover the wonder of the victorious Christian life.

A Whole New Walk and a Whole New Talk

Paul concluded this section of Ephesians with the desired result of grace: "For we are His workmanship, created in Christ Jesus for good works, which God prepared beforehand, that we should walk in them" (v. 10). We are not saved *by* works, we are saved *for* works. Grace gives us a whole new walk and a whole new talk. As God's masterpieces, we are portraits of grace on display for all to see.

Thus, we are not only saved by grace but we exist in it. Nothing can be done in the life of the Christian apart from the grace of God. All things are possible only by the grace of God—whether we work or play, marry or remain single. Grace is a mode of existence for the Christian. We should synchronize our whole lives around the grace of God.

Often people misunderstand grace. Rather than seeing it as a fertile bed of soil in which they can grow further, they treat the rich soil of God's grace as though it were dust. God did not rescue us from hell so that we could litter His marvelous generosity with indecent acts and bad attitudes. Grace frees us up to serve Him—not ourselves. Grace was not owed us by

God. His great plan of salvation originates "according to the counsel of His own will" (Eph. 1:11). God simply wanted to save us and so He did. Therefore, the life that we now lead should also be "according to the counsel of His own will."

THE SUFFICIENCY OF GRACE

The moment we became Christians, we were accepted in God's School of Grace. Our justification was just the introductory course to Grace 101. Throughout the rest of our earthly lives and throughout all eternity, we will be taking new courses in grace. What is important to note is that everything we will ever need to be all that God wants us to be has already been provided us by grace. The apostle Paul wrote, "And God is able to make all grace abound toward you, that you, always having all sufficiency in all things, may have an abundance for every good work" (2 Cor. 9:8).

And Paul continually referred to that abundance. In Ephesians 1:3, he said, "Blessed be the God and Father of our Lord Jesus Christ, who has blessed us with every spiritual blessing in heavenly places in Christ." It is important to observe that Paul is giving praise for blessings we already have, and these blessings are so comprehensive, they encompass everything.

Our challenge is not to ask God to bless us *but to lay hold of what we already possess.* God opened up an account in the Bank of Grace for you and me. In that account, He placed all the spiritual resources He would ever bestow upon us. Our responsibility is to make withdrawals. Far too many Christians live like spiritual paupers when they are actually spiritual millionaires.

Many people misinterpret spiritual blessings. They categorize these blessings into so-called spiritual areas—church, prayer, inner peace, witnessing. Instead spiritual blessings refer to God's comprehensive provisions for every aspect of our lives, since once we come to Christ everything becomes spiritual. As Paul noted elsewhere, "Whether you eat or drink or whatever you do, do all to the glory of God" (1 Cor. 10:31).

The implication of this truth is staggering. Nothing is left out. If you don't believe me, read through the long list below. As you do so, claim each spiritual blessings as your own:

- We are blessed with every spiritual blessing in heaven. Eph. 1:3.
- We are *always* led in His triumph (whether it appears so or not). 2 Cor. 2:14.
- We are equal members of His body (not inferior to other members). Eph. 5:30.
- Our hearts and minds are guarded by the peace of God. (Peace is *knowing* something, not always *feeling* it.) Phil. 4:7.
- We have all our needs (not greed) supplied. Phil. 4:19.
- We are seated in heaven (already)! Eph. 2:6.
- We have boldness and confident access to God. Eph. 3:12.
- We have wisdom, righteousness, sanctification, redemption. 1 Cor. 1:30.
- We are created for good performance ("And I can let Christ live through me to perform it"). Eph. 2:10.
- We have been brought near to God by Christ. Eph. 2:13.

- We are new creatures. (Even though we don't always feel or act like it, our deep desire is to be so.) 2 Cor. 5:17.
- We are the righteousness of God. (You can't get more righteous than this, brother!) 2 Cor. 5:21.
- We are liberated. Gal. 2:4.
- We are joined with all believers. Gal. 3:28.
- We are sons and heirs. Gal. 4:7.
- We are justified and redeemed (already!). Rom. 3:24.
- Our old self was killed (crucified). Rom. 6:6.
- We are free from the law of sin and death. Rom. 8:2.
- We are accepted. Rom. 15:7.
- We are sanctified (holy, set apart). 1 Cor. 1:2.
- We are chosen, holy and blameless before God. Eph. 1:4.
- We are forgiven. Eph. 1:7.
- We *have* obtained an inheritance. Eph. 1:10, 11.
- We are sealed with the Spirit. Eph. 1:13.
- We are alive (formerly we were dead). Eph. 2:5.
- We are raised up with Him. Col. 3:1.
- Our life is hidden with Christ in God. Col. 3:3.

This is just the beginning! The Bible is filled with other blessings that are ours *now*.

Why, then, are so many Christians defeated? Because spiritual blessings by their very nature are located in heavenly places. Far too many Christians hang out in earthly places and are therefore experiencing earthly results: defeat!

When we become Christians, we are immediately seated with Christ in heavenly places. Now! Even though we are still physically living on earth, our new life perspective is to be heavenly and eternal rather than earthly and temporal. It is for this reason we are to "seek those things which are above, where Christ is, . . . not on things on the earth" (Col. 3:1, 2).

Spiritual victory can only be achieved when we live our lives in accordance with a divine or heavenly frame of reference. As long as we think and act in accordance with this world, we deny ourselves access to our heavenly account in the Bank of Grace and are limited to getting our blessing from this world. That bank account will always come up marked: Insufficient Funds.

The question is: What will man do with the gift of God's grace?

WHAT WILL MAN DO WITH THE GIFT OF GOD'S GRACE?

Grace is not static. It is the active energy of God that enables Christians to be all we were called to be when Christ saved us. Yet grace demands responsibility at the same time it rejects human merit. The pearls of grace are far too precious for God to dispense them to those who will not handle them responsibly.

The concept of proper works is clearly set forth in 1 Corinthians 15. Paul, explaining the impact of grace in his own life said, "by the grace of God I am what I am." Christianity's greatest biblical author, missionary, evangelist, theologian, Bible teacher, and church architect says in essence, "These achievements were made by grace."

However, these achievements were not made by Paul idly sitting back, doing nothing. He went on to say, "But I labored more abundantly than they all, yet not I, but the grace of God which was with me" (vs. 10).

Note the tension. Paul labored and grace labored. Thus there is a dynamic cooperation between what grace provides and what we must do. Grace provides the soil out of which the fruit of the Spirit grows. This is why Paul was proud of the fact that the grace he had received from God was not given in vain (see 1 Cor. 15:10). The grace of God in Paul's life and ministry reaped a full harvest and was not cut short, hindered, or limited. So it should be in the life of every Christian.

You are a spiritual millionaire. God has opened an account for you in the Bank of Grace. What are you going to do with God's gift to you? The choice is yours.

3

THE ASSISTANT COACH:
THE ENABLEMENT OF
THE HOLY SPIRIT

SUPPOSE YOU WENT to Sears and purchased a brand new refrigerator, the top of the line. This model has all the bells and whistles and cost you a hefty $6,000. On your way home you stop at your local grocery store to purchase the food for your new appliance. Later that afternoon your refrigerator is delivered and installed, and you fill it with all the goodies you purchased—your favorite chocolate chip ice cream, chocolate milk, and fresh corn on the cob.

You retire for the night, but when you come into the kitchen the next morning, you experience the shock of your life. Ice cream is all over the floor! The milk is sour, and the vegatables are changing color! It is quickly evident that your brand new, top-of-the-line refrigerator isn't working!

Angry and disgusted you call Sears to give them a peace of your "Christian mind" for selling you a dud.

The salesperson who sold you the refrigerator is aghast at the news. He asks you to pull open the freezer door to see if the light comes on.

You do so. No light.

He then asks you to put your ear to the bottom of the refrigerator to see if you hear the low hum of the motor.

You do so. No hum.

Finally he asks you to look behind the refrigerator and see if the electrical cord has been plugged in.

You do so. Lo and behold the cord is lying on the floor, unplugged!

You return to the phone and inform the salesman that the refrigerator is unplugged but that shouldn't matter. You argue that for $6,000 it should work—plugged in or not!

The salesman then explains a very important principle to you—namely, refrigerators are dependent appliances. They were never made to work on their own. They are built with certain specifications that can only be realized when they have been energized by the power of electricity. While all the necessary parts are there, they will not work until they get the necessary electrical juice to enable them to be and do what they were created to do.

In this regard, Christians are like appliances. We are dependent creatures. When you receive Christ as Savior, He gives you the requisite parts necessary for you to live a victorious Christian life. But you will not be able to do so until you are plugged into God's power source: the Holy Spirit. Even though your new nature provides all the parts necessary to live a vibrant Christian life, you will find one part of your life after another perishing because the power to keep you operating as an alive and victorious child of God is absent.

THE PERSON OF THE HOLY SPIRIT

The term *Holy Spirit* reveals some apparent, though critical, truths.

First, the Holy Spirit is a spirit, not an it. That means he is non-material. He can't be touched or grabbed. He is beyond our five senses. He is vitally real, but must be spiritually perceived. That's why Jesus said, "The world cannot receive [Him], because it neither sees Him nor knows Him; . . . for He dwells with you and will be in you" (John 14:17). To put it more simply, if you are ever going to fully fathom the person of the Holy Spirit, you must be a spiritual being—a regenerated believer.

God's Spirit is often confused with the "force" referred to in the Star Wars movies—He becomes nothing more than a glorified energy field. But the Bible is very clear; the Holy Spirit is more than a power; He's a *powerful person.*

People who chase after "it" seek only the power that the Spirit has to offer, not the relationship. In Acts 8:9–25, we read about Simon, the magician, a Samaritan convert who saw God's power displayed as the apostles prayed and laid their hands on members of the congregation. Simon offered money to Peter and John and asked, "Give me this power also, that anyone on whom I lay my hands may receive the Holy Spirit."

The apostles replied, "Your money perish with you." God's Spirit is not on the market.

Pseudo-religious rip-off artists make their living by trying to package God's power for sale. They build a lucrative business, selling prayer cloths, water from the river Jordan, and splinters from the cross of Christ. (If you reassembled these "authentic" splinters, you'd have a cross as tall as the World Trade Center!) These "symbols of power" can be bought cheap. But God isn't offering symbols; He invites us into relationship with a powerful person.

Second, the Holy Spirit's name tells us that He is holy. The word *holy* means "set apart"—in this case, set apart from sin. Can you imagine how the Spirit reacts to living inside a believer who is not living right? He is holy!! No wonder He makes a reverberating frontal assault on our consciences.

His name tells us these two things. The Bible tells us a third. The Holy Spirit is part of the Trinity.

The Law Firm of God, God, and God

In a large law firm many of the attorneys specialize in different areas of law. When your case involves an area your attorney doesn't handle, he calls the lawyer in the next office. Chances are there will be a partner with the expertise to deal with whatever need you have.

Christians deal with a "law firm" of sorts, a partnership called "God, God, and God"—the Trinity (or the Godhead) made up of the Father, the Son, and the Holy Spirit. Only one firm, with three coequal partners. The Father determines the agenda for our lives; He sets the direction. The Son's job is to communicate the Father's mandate to us through the example of His life, and by direct instructions, such as the Great Commission. That's why the Bible calls Jesus the Word of God. The task of the Holy Spirit is implementation, as we shall soon see.

Thus, *the plan of the Father is communicated by the Son and implemented by the Spirit.* In this chapter we will look at the specific functions of the Holy Spirit.

THE PURPOSE OF THE HOLY SPIRIT

After Jesus died on the cross, the disciples were a ragamuffin, disorganized band. Christ was dead. Their faith was nearly dead. Then Jesus rose from the dead, and He met with the disciples. He promised to send the Holy Spirit to be with them, "to the end of the earth." That made a significant difference to the disciples—and it makes just as great a difference to us. Let's look at the ways the Holy Spirit works in each of our lives.

1. As a Comforter, an Enabler

Jesus promised to send a "comforter" to the disciples.

The word *comforter* is a somewhat weak and often misunderstood translation of a powerful Greek word. The original term, *paraclete,* means "one called alongside to enable."

What does the Spirit do? He enables us to be all that God has saved us to be and to do. He is not the kind of comforter who simply pats us on the back and encourages us when we're feeling low. He actually empowers us to carry out God's will. In other words, He gives us the backbone to live and to proclaim the truth.

Remember Peter? He was like a lot of Christians. Peter got caught up in the emotionalism of a great moment and told Jesus, "No matter what anyone else does, I will remain faithful." (See Matt. 26:33.) Of course, in a matter of hours, Peter's resolve crumbled, and he denied Christ three times—in very strong language.

A few short months later, Peter was a changed man. He was preaching to a crowd of thousands, boldly proclaiming the Lord before a skeptical audience.

What made the difference? In Acts 1:8, Jesus explained the metamorphosis: "But you shall receive power when the Holy Spirit has come upon you; and you shall be witnesses to Me in Jerusalem, and in all Judea and Samaria, and to the end of the earth." Peter had a paraclete!

Let me describe a paraclete in terms many can understand. The story is told of a little boy who was the favorite target of a neighborhood bully. Day after day, the boy was attacked and beaten up. His father advised him to stand up to the bully. The boy tried . . . and took a pounding as a result.

The next day, as the boy walked home, the bully stepped out from behind some bushes, took one look at his intended victim, and ran away as fast as he could. Why? The boy wasn't alone. His father was walking with him. In the flesh, the boy was helpless. But when his father "came alongside to enable" him, he had the confidence of a lion.

The Holy Spirit stands beside us, ready to deliver whatever support we may require in order to successfully live for Christ.

2. As a Reminder of Spiritual Truth

Do you recall your pastor's sermon from one year ago? How about last month? Last week?

Though it's enough to break a pastor's heart, the truth is most people forget what they've heard from the pulpit with alarming speed. It's no wonder, given the amount of data bombarding our minds each day.

That's why we so desperately need the Holy Spirit.

Jesus, in the process of warning His disciples about the persecution awaiting them, made this promise: "And you will be brought before governors and kings for My sake, as a testimony to them and to the Gentiles. But when they deliver you up, do not worry about how or what you should speak. For it will be given to you in that hour what you should speak; for it is not you who speak, but the Spirit of your Father who speaks in you" (Matt. 10:19–20).

The Spirit reminds us of all Jesus said to us. (See John 14:26.) It doesn't matter how many notes we take or how many verses we memorize. While both are important disciplines, ultimately it is the Holy Spirit who delivers that data to the front of our minds when we need it most.

As the New Testament unfolds, we see this promise fulfilled for Peter, Paul, Steven, and many others. And when the need arises—whether in a time of crisis or opportunity—it will be fulfilled for us.

3. As a Glorifier of Jesus

The job of the Holy Spirit is to glorify (to make known) Jesus Christ. The Lord said, "He will glorify Me, for He will take of what is mine and declare it to you. All things that the Father has are Mine" (John 16:14–15).

The Holy Spirit accomplishes this assignment in four basic ways: by inspiring and illuminating the Bible, by bringing people to Christ, by reproducing Christ's character in Christians, and by enabling us to serve Jesus. Let's look at each of those tasks.

By Inspiring and Illuminating the Bible. In John 16:12, 13, Jesus told His disciples, "I still have many things to say to you, but you cannot bear them now. However, when

He, the Spirit of truth has come, He will guide you into all truth; for He will not speak on His own authority, but whatever He hears He will speak; and He will tell you things to come."

Second Timothy 3:16 tells us that all Scripture is inspired, or "God-breathed." That means that my Bible is more than a book. It is the direct product of the Spirit of God.

Now, you may say, "Wait a minute. Men wrote this book and men are fallible. They forget, they make mistakes, they lose direction. So this book has errors in it!"

As far as I'm concerned, this notion that the Bible contains mistakes is . . . well, a mistake.

Second Peter 1:21 tells us, "prophecy never came by the will of man, but holy men of God spoke as they were moved by the Holy Spirit."

So you're partly right. Men wrote the Bible. Men are fallible, they forget, they make mistakes. But who was in charge of that writing project? God's Holy Spirit and He is infallible. He doesn't forget anything and has never made a mistake. Now the Bible tells us that when those apostles picked up the pen to write, the Holy Spirit crossed the *t*'s and dotted the *i*'s.

These men were "carried along" by the Spirit, much the same way a sailboat is carried along by the wind. You may be standing at the helm with a firm grip on the wheel, but once the wind begins to blow, there's no use deciding to travel in the opposite direction. You go where the wind carries you. Period.

The biblical writers held the pen; God authored the text. From Genesis 1:1 to the last verse in the Book of Revelation, from "pillar to post" and from cover to cover, this book is the absolute, uncompromising, authoritative, inerrant Word of God.

What the Spirit authored, He also illuminates. The Bible is a supernatural book so it takes supernatural understanding to recognize and apply its truth.

Paul digs into this weighty concept in 1 Corinthians 2:10–12: "The Spirit searches all things, yes, the deep things of God. For what man knows the things of a man except the spirit of the man which is in him? Even so, no one knows the things of God except the Spirit of God. Now, we have received not the spirit of the world, but the Spirit who is from God, that we might know the things that have been freely given to us by God."

Contained between the covers of your Bible are the very thoughts of God. And His Spirit within us enables us to grasp those thoughts and turn those spiritual principles into life-changing action.

By Bringing People to Christ. Jesus explained this task of the Holy Spirit to His disciples. He told them, "When He has come, He will convict the world of sin, and of righteousness, and of judgment: of sin, because they do not believe in Me; of righteousness, because I go to My Father and you see Me no more; of judgment, because the ruler of this world is judged" (John 16:8–10). He is an integral process of our salvation, which we talked about in the last chapter.

Thirdly, the Holy Spirit reproduces Christ's character in Christians.

By Reproducing Christ's Character in Christians. Have you ever watched a person try to break a bad habit? Smoking, nail-biting—whatever it might be—has become natural and automatic. And it takes enormous amounts of willpower and energy to fight those urges. Doing so is uncomfortable and unnatural.

That, however, is easy compared to the plight of a sinner who tries to stop sinning. It's almost like clamping a lid on a pot of boiling water. Either the lid must come off, or an explosion will occur.

The Holy Spirit offers believers a way to turn off the heat. He actually changes the power of the attitudes and desires that fuel our behavior.

Paul talked about the power of the Holy Spirit to change our lives in Romans 8: "If the Spirit of Him who raised Jesus from the dead dwells in you, He who raised Christ from the dead will also give life to your mortal bodies through His Spirit who dwells in you" (Rom. 8:11).

The "body of death" Paul referred to is irreparable. We can do nothing to make the flesh in which we live less prone to sin. We're stuck in these shells until we die.

The source of our sin problem is deep within each of us; it is "internal." That's why God chose to concentrate His solution on that very location. If you have accepted the Lord Jesus Christ as your Savior, God has literally taken up residence within you in the person of His Spirit.

There's a "down" side and an "up" side to this. First, the down side. Your excuses no longer hold water. You say you don't have the strength to avoid temptation? The Bible says, "He who is in you is greater than he who is in the world" (1 John 4:4). You say you feel far from God? How far could you be from your own insides?

That brings us back to the major theme of this book: All the power you need to do whatever God calls you to do is resident within you. This, of course, is the good news.

Have you ever watched a television news crew at work? You don't see the cameraman hunting for an electrical outlet as a breaking story is unfolding before him. Instead, he carries a battery pack around his waist, which enables him to film an event on a moment's notice. He doesn't have to hunt for power; he's got it with him. In the same way, Christians need not search for a source of power to deal with their sin. Their "battery pack" is internal—and it never powers down.

Without the work of the Holy Spirit, the apostle Paul could not have said, "It is God who works in you both to **will** and to do for His good pleasure" (Phil. 2:13).

Finally, the Holy Spirit enables us to serve Christ.

By Enabling Us to Serve Jesus Christ. No matter what assignment we might face in life, there is no substitute for being called to serve Jesus Christ. Luke gives us an example of this in the book of Acts: "As they ministered to the Lord and fasted, the Holy Spirit said, 'Now separate to Me Barnabus and Saul for the work which I have called them' " (Acts 13:2). There's no stopping the man or woman whom the Holy Spirit has singled out for service.

When I made the decision to organize Oak Cliff Bible Fellowship (the Dallas church that I pastor), I had a very small salary, but a very big calling. I eagerly worked as many as seventy-five hours per week because God had called me to the work.

You see, when a man is called, it doesn't matter how much opposition you stir up against him. He knows God will make a way somehow because he's called. He wrestles with his problems joyfully because he's called.

Ultimately, he emerges from the fray successful and triumphant because he's called.

How does the Holy Spirit equip you for this kind of success? By providing "spiritual gifts"—supernatural abilities, sensitivities, and inclinations that empower believers to build up the Body, overcome obstacles, and press on to success in obedience.

What kinds of gifts will God give you? That depends on the job He has called you to do. Paul talked about these gifts in 1 Corinthians: "There are diversities of gifts, but the same Spirit. There are differences of ministries, but the same Lord. And there are diversities of activities, but it is the same God who works all in all" (1 Cor. 12:4–6).

God has every angle covered. He provides the job, the "service" (in my case, the pastorate); the strategy, the "kinds of working" (in my case, a long range plan of staffing and outreach to the local community); and the tools, "gifts" (my persistence, my ability to speak God's Word forcefully). All that remains is for us to be willing to get to work.

Now that you've gotten to know the Holy Spirit and His tasks within the Trinity, I'd like you to take a self-test, a tool to let you know if you are filled with Holy Spirit power.

ARE YOU FILLED WITH HOLY SPIRIT POWER?

If you look up on a clear day, you can sometimes see vapor trails streaking across the sky. A jet has flown overhead. The aircraft may be too high to see, but the vapor trail is proof positive that it was there.

In the same way, the Holy Spirit leaves an unmistakable trail. If He is active and at work within us, there are five very obvious clues. Do these clues identify you as a Spirit-filled believer? (Check the ones that apply to you.)

Clue #1. You become a witness about the person and works of Jesus Christ.

After rising from the dead and shortly before ascending into heaven, Jesus said to His disciples, "You shall receive power when the Holy Spirit has come upon you; and you shall be witnesses to Me in Jerusalem, and in all Judea and Samaria, and to the end of the earth" (Acts 1:8). Notice that He did *not* say, "You will *do* witnessing." Jesus was not describing an activity; He was foretelling a dramatic change from within.

Not long after, on the day of Pentecost, these same disciples were given the ability to speak in languages they had not learned and found themselves proclaiming Christ to an assembly of foreigners. Their behavior was unnatural; the crowd supposed them drunk. Peter (who had developed a reputation for putting his foot in his mouth and had denied Christ three times, as I mentioned in the last chapter) quoted Scripture and proclaimed the good news. The results were recorded in Acts 2:41: "About three thousand were added to them." A clear case of Holy-Spirit intoxication!

If you are truly under the influence of the Spirit, you are going to talk about Jesus. Nothing will intimidate you; no person or circumstance will stop you. It will not be the kind of task you simply grit your teeth and bear. It will be a joyful expression of who you *are*: a witness.

Clue #2. Those who are filled with the Spirit worship God.

Paul instructed the Ephesian Christians: "Be filled with the Spirit, speaking to one another in psalms and hymns and spiritual songs, singing and making melody in your heart to the Lord, giving thanks always for all things to God the Father, in the name of our Lord Jesus Christ" (Eph. 5:18–20).

That short passage is loaded with examples of worship, both public and private. The Spirit-filled believer doesn't have to be enticed into worship; he can't help but worship. He doesn't have to be coaxed into going to church; he can't wait to be among God's people. He needn't be goaded into prayer; he thrives on communicating with his heavenly Father.

Imagine a bucket filled with water. The moment the bucket is moved, the water spills out, drenching the objects surrounding it. When we are full of the Spirit, "living water" inevitably spills out of our singing mouths, our dancing feet, and our clapping hands. Those around us are refreshed by the splash! For the Spirit-led believer, worshipping, like witnessing, is an automatic expression of who we are.

Clue #3. There is mutual submission within the body.

Typically, interpersonal relationships are driven by one common motivation: selfishness. Everybody's in it for himself. Divorce, sibling rivalry, job stress—even war—are the result of somebody (or a group of somebodies) not getting his way. However, as your focus in life shifts away from your own fleshly desires and toward Christ, doing it "my way" becomes less important than doing it "Christ's way."

Paul told the Ephesian Christians: "[Submit] to one another in the fear of God" (Eph. 5:21).

The best example of submission in the Bible (and in human history, for that matter) is Jesus Christ.

Jesus poured His deity into a shell of humanity in order to come to earth and become your servant. "Being in the form of God, [He] did not consider it robbery to be with God, but made Himself of no reputation, taking the form of a servant, and coming in the likeness of men. And being found in appearance as a man He humbled Himself and became obedient to the point of death, even the death of the cross" (Phil. 2:6–8).

According to the apostle Paul who described Jesus in this way, this should be our attitude: "Let nothing be done through selfish ambition or conceit," he said, "but in lowliness of mind let each esteem others better than himself" (Phil. 2:3).

In Ephesians 6 Paul portrayed what will happen when we submit to one another as the Spirit enables. Wives submit to their husbands. Husbands, in turn, love their wives and put the needs of their family ahead of their own. Children become obedient. Parents remain sensitive and responsive to their youngsters' physical, spiritual, and emotional needs. Slaves (employees) respect their masters (employers) out of reverence for Christ, and employers remember that their Master in heaven shows no favoritism to masters over slaves.

The Holy Spirit gives us the ability to set aside our own agenda and devote our energy and attention to serving one another, thus advancing the cause of Christ.

Clue # 4. The Spirit-filled believer bears spiritual fruit. If a fruit tree is alive and healthy, you don't have to coax it to produce fruit. It can't help but do that. In Galatians 5:22, Paul described the harvest we naturally yield when we're rooted in the Spirit:

- *Love.* Not "butterflies in the stomach." That's Hollywood love. Biblical love is selflessly seeking the will of God for the one you love.
- *Joy.* The inner contentment we experience despite our external circumstances.
- *Peace.* Harmony in our human relationships.
- *Patience.* Most people think patience is passive, that it only refers to waiting; but patience also involves our ability to endure and our ability to forgo an inpatient response when we are justly provoked. Patience is active; it means surrendering our right to hurt back when others hurt us.
- *Kindness and goodness.* These synonyms have different shades of meaning; however, they both connote loving treatment of those who don't deserve it.
- *Faithfulness.* This means reliability in service; the kind of dependable commitment God can count on.
- *Gentleness* (or meekness). The ability to submit yourself to the will of God. The strongest man is not the one who forces his will upon others but the man who has that power and willingly surrenders it.
- *Self-control.* The ability to resist fleshly impulses.

All of this spiritual fruit blossoms spontaneously in the Spirit-controlled believer. That's why Paul said, "If you are led by the Spirit, you are not under the law"

(Gal. 5:18). Rules are for those who live in the flesh; they do what is right because right is enforced. Those who live by the Spirit do what is right because it pleases God.

Many of you wives probably experienced this kind of motivation during the early days of your marriage. You cooked, you cleaned, and you laundered because you wanted to please your man. You wanted him well-fed, sparkling clean, and tidy. Nothing was too good, no sacrifice too great for your beloved hunk of masculinity.

That was then.

A few years downstream, something changed—and it wasn't your list of chores. Your motivation shifted. Today, you cook because he'll bellow if he gets hungry. You clean because you can't stand a filthy house. You do laundry because you don't want your children seen in public in dirty clothes.

One scenario describes living by the Spirit, the other illustrates living by law.

Clue #5. Spirit-controlled Christians are dynamically involved in service for Christ.

Some Christians treat these manifestations (or gifts) as "merit badges" and brandish them boldly to demonstrate how spiritual they are. Those who are truly Spirit-filled understand that the Spirit empowers us for a purpose, namely to serve other Christians by enabling them to progress in their spiritual lives. Paul told the Corinthian Christians: "But the manifestation of the Spirit is given to each one for the profit of all" (1 Cor. 12:7). If you only use your gifts and talents for your own purposes, the Spirit is not controlling you.

How Did You Score?

If my description of the Spirit-filled life seems foreign and unfamiliar to you, I urge you to reevaluate your directions and priorities before pressing on down the path. Pray about your spiritual condition and, if you can, talk further with your pastor or a Spirit-filled Christian friend.

You say, "I'd like this battery pack to come alongside me. How does that happen?"

HOW TO TURN ON THE HOLY SPIRIT BATTERY PACK

Once you accept Jesus Christ, the Spirit indwells you automatically. But in Ephesians Paul suggested that the Spirit does not automatically *fill* you. He told the early Christians, "Do not be drunk with wine, in which is dissipation; but be filled with the Spirit" (Eph. 5:18).

In the Greek, the verb *fill* is in the present imperative tense, which denotes a continuous condition, an ever-present command. Though the Holy Spirit's power is contained within you, you must activate Him. This process is called the "filling of the Spirit." But how does it work? Well, Paul likened it to being drunk with wine. Let's explore that analogy.

Liquor transforms a person. For example, a quiet man may get loud if he's drunk. One who can't sing might bellow great songs. A passive man might become violent. A person who is afraid of his shadow may suddenly believe he can fight Mike Tyson. No wonder people often say after sobering up, "I don't know what got into me." Well, *I* know what got into them: alcohol. And alcohol changes people from what they are into something totally different.

Note also that in order to get drunk, a person *must* drink. It doesn't occur accidently or by hoping. It is the result of following through with an act of will.

Once under the influence, the drunk person's speech is affected. He or she can no longer walk a straight line. He makes different decisions and experiences different perceptions. Why? Because he is no longer being controlled by his own mind, but by the substance at work within him. In short, he acts unnatural.

"Instead," Paul said, "be filled with the Holy Spirit." People under the influence of the Holy Spirit also behave in unnatural ways. Those with violent tempers develop self-control. Those dominated by greed learn generosity. Those given to immorality gain the upper hand on their urges. Hate gives way to love, stubbornness to understanding, and dissension to unity. Totally unnatural!

God wants His Spirit to control the way we walk, talk, think, and act. He wants to work from within us to glorify Christ. There is no question that each of us will be "under the influence." We are either controlled by the flesh or by the Spirit. It is up to us to choose the Spirit and start "drinking." If the Holy Spirit is dwelling dormantly inside you, you may be asking, "How do I turn the key?" You turn on the battery pack by just asking God to fill you with His Spirit.

And your next question is naturally, "Now that the engine is on, how can I cover some distance on this highway toward victorious Christian living?"

HOW TO LIVE DAILY IN THE POWER OF THE SPIRIT

Paul also gave the early Christians advice on how to live in the power of the Holy Spirit. Let him speak to you directly through his words.

1. *"Do not grieve the Holy Spirit of God, by whom you were sealed for the day of redemption"* (Eph. 4:30).

Let me tell you about the Holy Spirit. He's very sensitive emotionally; He gets upset quickly. In fact, the image of the Holy Spirit in the Bible is that of a dove—a very sensitive bird.

What makes the Holy Spirit sensitive? Sin. We grieve the Holy Spirit when, instead of moving toward righteousness, we entertain *unrighteousness.* That's why verse 31 of Ephesians went on to say, "Let all bitterness, wrath, anger, clamor, and evil speaking be put away from you with all malice."

Grieving the Holy Spirit has much the same result as grieving a sensitive wife—it disrupts the fellowship you share. An errant husband shouldn't expect a shower of hugs and kisses from a wounded spouse. Similarly, a believer immersed in unrighteousness can't expect comfort and support from a grieved Holy Spirit.

2. *"Do not quench the Spirit"* (1 Thess. 5:19).

"Do not put out the Spirit's fire," says the New International Version of the Bible. The Holy Spirit's job is to build a fire of faith within you. But just as the embers start heating up, some of us run for the hose.

Once we yield control to the Spirit, He works to sensitize our conscience. He gives us a renewed awareness of right and wrong. The more heat He generates, the more acute that awareness becomes.

Quenching the Spirit—rationalizing away or openly defying His direction—wounds the conscience. Eventually, scar tissue begins to build up. The voice of the Spirit becomes inaudible through that tissue, which causes the line between right and wrong to grow blurry and eventually impossible to discern.

"Do not grieve the Holy Spirit," Paul advised. "Do not quench the Spirit." And finally, Paul told the early Christians to "walk by the Spirit."

3. *"Walk in the Spirit, and you shall not fulfill the lust of the flesh"* (Gal. 5:16).

How do you make progress in the faith? Walk. Don't leap, don't run—walk.

When I walk, I move forward by committing my weight fully to one leg, then to the other.

Once, during a football game, I broke my right leg in two places. After surgery, my leg was set in a cast and I was given a pair of crutches, which were able to support the weight my leg could no longer carry. Walking, then, was simply one act of dependency after another.

As we try to live this Christian life on our own, we find our legs can't hold us up. The flesh is not strong enough. But God has given us the crutches of the Holy Spirit. So instead of depending on your leg of flesh and collapsing to the floor, you can rest your spiritual weight on the crutch of the Holy Spirit. (If He can create the world and keep it in place, He can certainly support and direct you!)

We exercise this dependency on the Spirit through prayer. If each step we take and each decision we make is rooted in prayer, we are depending on the Spirit and not our flesh to live the victorious Christian life.

During the days of my football injury, I had another crutch: my wife. Whenever I needed to climb the stairs, Lois would bend down and help me lift the heavy cast up to the next step. If I needed to hobble from place to place, I put my arm around her for support. She bore my weight as I stumbled along.

We need to add this last image to our understanding of the Holy Spirit. He is there, alongside us, fully capable of bearing our weight, no matter how much of a burden we might be. He's like my wife in the sense that all the while He loves us. As He carries us along, He softly whispers words of encouragement. He's sensitive to our sore spots. (We're not dealing with a real crutch, which is only a stick of wood.) The Holy Spirit is a person, eager to relate to us tenderly and intimately.

Let the Spirit come alongside you and enable you as you face every issue in your life. God has given you an expensive million dollar appliance—your body. And He's added the billion dollar power of the Holy Spirit to make it function successfully. It's up to you to plug into that Power.

4

LOST SPIRITUAL YARDAGE: THE CANCER OF CARNALITY

CANCER IS A dreaded disease. It begins when one cell no longer wants to go along with the body's program and decides to go solo, to do its own thing. Not only does this cell begin to act independently, it also begins reproducing its own kind. One rebellious cell begets a whole new family of Benedict Arnolds, producing a lump in some part of the body, which instead of contributing to the body begins to rob the body of its strength. As if this weren't bad enough, these traitors then decide to metastasize, spreading their influence to other parts of the body. Like the Mafia, they silently, yet violently, penetrate vital organs to establish their own cronies and sabotage each organ's effectiveness. If undiagnosed or left untreated, this army of rebels brings death and destruction to the whole body.

Similarly, a spiritual cancer is destroying the effectiveness of the church in the world. The effects of this disease are clearly evident in the high divorce rate of Christian couples, the immorality among Christian leaders, the lack of spiritual power and ineffective testimony among Christians, and many other maladies of spiritual defeat. The formal name of this spiritual cancer is *carnality*. Just as cancer is abnormal for the body so carnality is abnormal in the life of the Christian. It cannot go untreated without catastrophic results.

God, our Heavenly Father, has adopted us, granted us a new life and an eternal inheritance through His only begotten Son, Jesus Christ. But many of His children have become rebellious, wayward children. You may be one who has become a spiritual runaway. Your sins have increased the gulf between you and a Holy God. That's why you feel He doesn't hear you, that's why you feel so alone.

So what spiritual team do you represent? Satan's or God's? Paul talked about four types of Christians in his first epistle to the mostly carnal Corinthian church: the natural man, the spiritual man, the baby Christian, and the carnal Christian.

THE NATURAL MAN

The first type of person is the natural man. Paul said, "But the natural man does not receive the things of the Spirit of God; for they are foolishness to him; nor can he know them, because they are spiritually discerned" (1 Cor. 2:14).

Notice that the natural man has two problems. First, he does not accept the things of the Spirit because he considers them foolishness. Second and far worse, however, is the fact that he cannot understand them.

If your child comes home with a poor mark on an exam for which he did not study, that's one thing. If the teacher calls you in for a conference and informs you that your child lacks the capacity to learn, that is quite another.

As I watch the evening news, I see local, national, and global leaders applying natural human wisdom to monumental problems. Without the mind of Christ, it's no wonder their social programs fail, their justice systems falter, and their economic strategies become bankrupt. It's like trying to cure cancer with a Band-Aid. The world is stocked with an abundance of Band-Aids. What it lacks are biblical solutions.

In order to sense the distance between human intellect and divine wisdom, I suggest you read Isaiah 40. There, God essentially asked, "To whom can I be compared?" In thirty-one short verses, He made it abundantly clear who He is and who we are. If we compare His traits to our own intellect, we see how inept we really are.

For example, when was the last time the scientific community "stretched out the heavens like a curtain" (v. 22)? Or do you recall reading about any team from *National Geographic* that "measured heaven with a span, and calculated the dust of the earth by the measure, and weighed the mountains in a scale, and the hills in a balance" (v. 12)?

The natural man is just that, natural—like everyone else but unlike God because of the absence of God's Spirit in his life. The natural man is a non-Christian. He's like a man who doesn't have cable. He may have a big-screen, color television with a fancy remote, but he can't get certain movies. If you're a non-Christian, you may have money and power and prestige, but if you don't have the cable of Christ, you can't link into God's power.

I hear some Christians say, "Man, I've backslidden!"

Probably so. Then again, they may have never front-slidden. Let's get one thing straight: Carnal Christians and non-Christians aren't the same. If you're not saved, you're worse off. You're lost.

The second type of person is the spiritual man.

THE SPIRITUAL MAN

The spiritual man is a mature Christian. He thinks as Christ thinks. Although he doesn't do it perfectly, he consistently appraises, evaluates, and examines things from God's perspective. Paul told the Corinthian Christians: "But he who is spiritual judges all things, yet he himself is rightly judged by no one. For 'who has known the mind of the Lord that he may instruct Him?' But we have the mind of Christ" (1 Cor. 2:15–16). Kids, for example, don't think a lot about saving money because at their maturity level, they don't doesn't see long-term. But mature people do, looking not only at the moment, but at the future. So it is with a mature Christian, who connects present decisions with future consequences, focusing not only on the here-and-now but on eternity. That would make you a very unique individual, wouldn't it? Well, that is exactly the kind of person you are to become as you move toward spiritual maturity.

According to this verse, the only insight greater than that possessed by the spiritual man belongs to God Himself. Obviously, no one can teach the Lord anything, since He already knows everything. In His mind reside the knowledge and experience of eternity. The good news is, *we have the mind of Christ.* As spiritually mature Christians, God's all-knowing mind operates within us through Christ.

That means we are regenerated beings with the capacity to see all of life from a divine perspective! Don't be surprised if immature Christians and nonbelievers grumble, "What's wrong with him?" when you think this way. Expect them to ask, "Have you lost your mind, or do you just lack commonsense? Where's the logic in that idea? We've never done it that way before!" On and on they go—and that's perfectly natural. No one can share your vision if they cannot share your vantage point.

Next Paul describes the baby Christian.

THE BABY CHRISTIAN

The baby Christian is new to the faith, like an infant is new to life. He tells the Corinthians, "And I, brethren, could not speak to you as to spiritual people, but as to carnal, as to babes in Christ" (3:1).

If you're in a foreign country where people are speaking another language, you won't understand much. But you don't get too frustrated because you realize you're new to the environment. That's the way it is for a baby Christian. He doesn't understand all of the spiritual language. He walks and talks like a baby. But eventually he picks up more and more knowledge and matures (at least he should), based in part on his desire and effort. The immature Corinthian Christians were baby Christians; they had not had enough time in the faith to see many of the much-needed changes from their old lives.

The fourth type of person—the one we are focusing on in this chapter—is the carnal Christian.

THE CARNAL CHRISTIAN

The carnal Christian is a fleshly Christian. Even though you became a new creature when you were saved, you're still acting out fleshly patterns of behavior, Paul said (3:2, 3).

You are like a stalled car. Your driver is God; your engine, Jesus Christ; the gas, the Holy Spirit, and the road map, the Bible. But you are going nowhere—or even backwards because you're stuck in the mud of sin.

A carnal Christian is caught between two worlds. He believes Christ is real and genuinely believes in His sacrifice on the cross. Even so, he clings intentionally to his worldly ways. Though he is saved, he is still swayed by the propensity of his natural nature.

For such believers, Paul prescribed a diet of spiritual milk, the basic nourishment of the fundamentals of the faith.

Keep in mind that Paul first visited Corinth in about 50 A.D. He preached to the Corinthians, witnessed their salvation, and fed them this spiritual milk. About six years later, their spiritual diet was still composed of milk. (Consider the human equivalent: if you were still pumping pabulum down the throat of a five-year-old, you'd be long overdue for a visit to the doctor!) Just like an overgrown infant, a carnal Christian who fails to move toward maturity is a sick Christian, attempting to keep one foot planted in two mutually exclusive worlds.

Galatians 5:17 reminds us that the flesh and the Spirit are at war with one another. How can we ask the flesh and the Spirit to cohabit within us at the same time? It's like a man saying to his new bride, "Honey, I love you and I am so happy to be married to you. Oh, by the way, my mistress will be moving in with us on weekends. You don't mind, do you?" Any wife in her right mind would find that arrangement ludicrous. So does God!

Finally, notice how Paul concluded this passage. Because of their jealousies and internal bickering, Paul accused the Corinthians of being "mere men" or natural men. Most of our contemporaries would consider that high praise.

In our society, humanity is not only celebrated, it is worshipped under the banner of "humanism." All manners of immoral behavior become not only tolerable, but entirely acceptable. Premarital sex is "natural." Divorce is "unavoidable." Abortion is "only reasonable." Biblically speaking, however, it is a shameful thing to be a "mere man" when, through Christ, we are offered the opportunity to become spectacular, spiritual people, indwelt by the very mind of Christ.

Make no mistake. All of us commit sin (see Rom. 3:23). And if you say you don't, you just committed a sin called lying (1 John 1:8,10). Committed Christians may fall into sin, but a carnal Christian bathes in sin. He has the mind-set, motivation, and methodology of sin.

THE SPIRITUAL DISEASE OF CARNALITY

So what kind of spiritual disease is carnality? Who can catch it?

Simply defined, carnality *is a spiritual state in which a born-again Christian knowingly, willingly, intentionally, and persistently lives to please and serve self rather than Jesus Christ.* Many of us modify this definition in order to exclude ourselves or our friends. Instead, let's clarify this definition once and for all by looking for the characteristics of the disease. But first, let's consider and important point.

Believe It or Not, Carnal Christians Are Genuine Christians.

First of all, carnal Christians are genuine Christians. They have received Christ as Savior, but they are refusing to submit to Him and serve Him as Lord. They, not He, sit on the throne of their lives.

Yes, it's possible to be on your way to heaven but be of no earthly good because you compromise your faith. That a person can be a genuine Christian and be carnal is clear because Paul called the Corinthians brethren in 1 Corinthians 3:1. "And I, brethren, could not speak to you as to spiritual men, but as to carnal, as to babes in Christ." Paul believed that these Corinthian Christians were a part of the family of God. He also referred to them as "in Christ," leaving little doubt.

And in greeting them at the beginning of 1 Corinthians, he said, "To the church of God which is at Corinth, to those who are sanctified in Christ Jesus, called to be saints, with all who in every place call on the name of Jesus Christ our Lord."

The words *sanctified* and *saints* come from the same root word, which means "to be set apart" for God's purposes. And whenever the Bible uses the words *calling upon the name of the Lord Jesus Christ,* it refers to

Christians. As much as we'd like to think otherwise, Paul was referring to Christians.

If you still doubt that genuine Christians can be carnal, think about a few biblical characters. There was Saul, the king of Israel. The Bible says that God changed his heart (1 Sam. 10:9). Yet his rebellion against God led to witchcraft and ultimately suicide.

There was Solomon, a wise king. So committed was Solomon that in his dedicatory prayer as king, he said, "Don't give me riches, give me wisdom" (2 Chron. 1:1–13). Yet his life of carnality—because of his love for many women—led him to write about the emptiness of life in the Book of Ecclesiastes, as I already mentioned.

Then there were those bad boys of Jacob, who sold their own brother into slavery. And David, who committed adultery and murder and tried to hide it until the prophet Nathan confronted him.

The New Testament also has illustrations of Christians who became carnal. Hymenaeus and Alexander threw away their faith, according to 1 Timothy 1:20. Demos left Paul for "this present world." In fact Paul saw the members of the Corinthian church as carnal, rebellious Christians.

So it's possible to be spiritually victorious yesterday and spiritually defeated today. That's why we must keep short accounts with God and have a daily walk with God's Spirit (see Gal. 16). Otherwise, we run the real risk of becoming spiritual failures.

THE CHARACTERISTICS OF THE DISEASE

Have you ever been lost, and stubbornly refused to pull over and get proper directions? You made wrong turns into an unfamiliar, sometimes dangerous neighborhood. You drove in circles, passing the same landmarks. Then you ran out of gas!

That's what Christians do as they drive down the highway of carnality. Like Solomon, Christians drive into a neighborhood of debauchery. Like the sons of Jacob, Christians drive into an area of lying. Like Hymenaeus and Alexander, Christians throw away their faith just as a car runs out of gas (1 Tim. 1:20).

None of these biblical characters fell into carnality because they made one bad turn. They made many, many wrong turns that led to a poor spiritual driving record. Therefore, carnality is characterized by persistently regressing in your spiritual life.

So, like that ubiquitous television commercial, "This is a test." Take it! Examine yourself as you consider four characteristics of carnality, using the Book of Hebrews as your guide. Check the characteristics that apply to you or someone you love.

You Neglect Spiritual Matters.

The author of Hebrews, who included himself in the discussion, was writing to a group of Jewish Christians who had turned their backs on the faith. He raised a fundamental question, the first test down the road to carnality: "How shall we escape if you neglect so great a salvation" (Heb. 2:3)?

Neglect here simply means disinterest, passive disobedience. In other words, you're not planning to do wrong, but you're not doing the right things to catapult you down the road to spiritual maturity. For example, a student doesn't have to curse the teacher or get caught cheating on a test to fail. All he has to do is not study. If a marriage ends in divorce, it's not always because the husband beats his wife or commits adultery. He may have stared at the T.V. too long, stopped dating her, stopped opening doors and being courteous to her, stopped complimenting her. If a person is sick, it's not always because he's done destructive things to his body. He may have just neglected to eat properly.

Some Christians end up on the road to carnality because of such neglect. Satan lulls us into neglecting the word of God, staying off our knees in prayer.

Why? What causes us to "neglect so great a salvation?" The same reason we take people and things for granted: We forget the importance of what we have—or we never fully realized its value. It's like the wife who says: "My husband has gotten used to cooked meals and washed clothes and ironed shirts." Or the husband who says: "My wife's gotten used to me being a hard worker and sensitive, caring person." Both feel taken for granted. And so does God. He gives us His only begotten Son. He gives us eternal life. He gives us the enablement of the Holy Spirit. He gives us answers to prayer. He gives us cures for our hurting hearts. And He asks, "How can you neglect so great a salvation?"

Next, the carnal Christian is characterized by an increase in spiritual insensitivity.

You Have Become Spiritually Insensitive.

Paul warned the Hebrew Christians: "Beware, brethren, lest there be in any of you an evil heart of unbelief in departing from the living God; but exhort one another daily, while it is called Today, lest any one of you be hardened through the deceitfulness of sin" (Heb. 3:12–13).

Again, the use of *brethren* indicates the author was writing to Christians. He was also talking about people with hard hearts, people who while stealing a car kill the woman sitting in it. People who often say, "I don't care."

Many Christians are duped into a hard heart by "the deceitfulness of sin." Some young people are in jail because they stopped believing their father and mother and started believing the wrong kind of peers. And that's when parents say what God says to us: "If you would only listen to Me and stop listening to sin, your heart wouldn't be hard and you wouldn't be duped into a defeated life that goes nowhere."

How do you know if you've been duped? Simple. Sin bothers you less and less. Sin is like a woodpecker pecking at your life. When you look at the individual pecks, it's not all that bad. But when the pecking is over, you've got a gaping hole in the tree of your life.

On the other hand, the mature Christian views sin like a room full of air. He sees the sunbeams shine through the window and notices the particles of dust in a room that looks tidy at first glance. Whenever the light of Christ is shining in your life, you should be sensitive to the dust of sin in your heart.

Next, the carnal Christian is characterized by withdrawing from the fellowship of other Christians.

You Withdraw from the Fellowship of Other Christians.

You can tell you're on the road to carnality when you don't feel like going to church. Instead, you become a member of Mattress Methodist or Bedside Baptist. Yes, it's true you don't have to go to church to be a Christian, but you should go to church if you want to be a mature Christian. The author of Hebrews told the Christians, "Let us consider one another in order to stir up love and good works, not forsaking the assembling of ourselves together, as is the manner of some, but exhorting one another, and so much the more, as you see the Day approaching" (Heb. 10:24, 25). God wants you to receive dynamic motivation, fellowship, and teaching.

Lastly, the carnal Christian is characterized by rejection of the Christian faith.

You Reject the Christian Faith.

If we stay on the road to carnality, we will fall away from the faith. We will deny Christ in our words and works—and we will pay the price. Even Jesus' blood can't save us from the discipline of God. The author of Hebrews warned the Christians, "For if we sin willfully after we have received the knowledge of the truth, there no longer remains a sacrifice for sins, but a certain fearful expectation of judgment, and fiery indignation which will devour the adversaries" (Heb. 10:26–27).

The author was talking to believers. That's why he used *we* in verse 26, and reminded them in verse 32, "Recall the former days, in which, after you were illuminated." In other words, they had the light.

The second half of verse 32 says, "You endured a great struggle with sufferings." Why? Because you bore the reproach of Christ. How? "Partly while you were made a spectacle both by reproaches and tribulations, and partly while you became companions of those who were so treated" (v. 33).

The carnal life has consequences more far reaching than we'd like to believe.

THE CONSEQUENCES OF THE DISEASE

Living a carnal life is like the law of gravity: What goes up, must come down. So when you persistently and knowingly live for yourself rather than God, you can land hard on the pavement of life.

In short, if you're a carnal Christian, you risk severe judgment in time and eternity. Carnality can result in divine discipline.

Divine Discipline

So how bad is the punishment of rejection the author of Hebrews spoke about in chapter ten? He reflected on the severity in verse 29: "Of how much worse punishment, do you suppose, will he be thought worthy who has trampled the Son of God under foot, counted the blood of the covenant by which he was sanctified a common thing, and insulted the Spirit of grace?"

The writer of Hebrews also warned these early Christians: "You have forgotten the exhortation which speaks to you as to sons, 'My son, do not despise the chastening of the LORD, nor be discouraged when you are rebuked by Him; for whom the LORD loves He chastens, and scourges every son whom He receives' " (Heb. 12:5, 6).

Notice that you must be a child of God to receive His discipline. He calls you son. And since He loves you, He will spank you to correct your wrongs. In fact, the author wrote in verse 7, "If you endure chastening, God deals with you as with sons; for what son is there whom a father does not chasten?"

Now if God isn't disciplining you for your wrongs, you have a bigger problem. You're not saved. Verse 8 says so: "But if you are without chastening, of which all have become partakers, then you are illegitimate and not sons." If God doesn't discipline you on earth, God will do so in eternity.

Furthermore, there's a correlation between discipline and respect, as verse 9 says, "We have had human fathers who corrected us, and we paid them respect. Shall we not much more readily be in subjection to the Father of spirits and live?"

You may wonder how many licks God is going to give you. His response, found in verse 10, is much like that of most parents: "I will discipline you until you get the message." And don't forget, God doesn't make mistakes like parents. He knows when and why and how you did it, and whether you're thinking about doing it again. And sometimes it's going to hurt.

If you take a long vacation and forsake your rigorous weight-lifting regimen, it's going to hurt when you go back into the gym. Well, when you lay off Christ, it's going to be painful when God veers you back into the gym of life. His discipline could be sickness or financial hardship or any number of other unpleasant occurrances—and you won't have the joy or peace that faithful Christians receive during such trials.

Sometimes a mother will tell her kids, "Wait until your father comes home." It's bad when Mama hits you, but Lord have mercy on you when the powerful hand of Daddy pops you! That's what the author of Hebrews is saying in 10:31: "It is a fearful thing to fall into the hands of the living God."

So if you're on the road to carnality, going from bad to worse, you'd better get off at the next exit, cross over the bridge, and get back on the right road of God's will before "Big Daddy" comes home.

If you get the message of God's spanking, Hebrews 12:11 says, you will then enjoy "the peaceable fruit of righteousness." You'll be like the child who is told by a parent after a spanking, "I just want to let you know I love you." So does God.

The Lost Assurance of Salvation

I'm sure you've been wondering throughout this chapter, "Is Tony saying that I might lose my salvation? Isn't it scriptural to believe, 'Once saved, always saved'?"

Yes, . . . but. You can lose your assurance of that salvation.

To substantiate what I am saying, let's look at Peter's second letter to early Christians. He warned them, "For he who lacks these things is shortsighted, even to blindness, and has forgotten that he was cleansed from his old sins. Therfore, brethren, be even more diligent to make your calling and election sure, for if you do these things you will never stumble; for so an entrance will be supplied to you abundantly into the everlasting kingdom of our Lord and Savior Jesus Christ" (1:9–11).

Peter exhorted Christians to commit themselves to grow by applying various spiritual traits with diligence. There's no such thing as a neutral or cruising Christian. You are either a growing Christian or a carnal Christian. A Christian who forgets his "purification from his former sins" is usually one so into the world that he adopts Satan's lifestyle. God is not working in your life, so you lose the certainty, peace, and joy that goes with the knowledge of your salvation.

For instance, if I live a life my parents disapprove of, I am still their child. But I am going to wonder how well they will receive me if I go home to visit them. If I am living "Satan's lifestyle," as a carnal Christian, I am going to wonder if God will really want to see me when I go home to heaven—and may even fear He will reject me. But I'm still His child.

Physical Death

Carnality may even result in physical death. In the first few verses of 1 Corinthians 10, Paul reminded carnal Christians about the plight of Israel in the wilderness and of the spiritual benefits God gave them so they could be victorious. They ran headlong into the great Red Sea so God rolled back the waters to create a passageway; they experienced God's deliverance. They were in an uncharted desert so God gave them a cloud to lead them by day and a pillar of fire to guide them by night; they experienced His guidance. They were in a desolate, barren land without plants or animals to eat so God gave them manna, spiritual food; they experienced His provision. They even had Christ in the Old Testament, for verse 4 says, "They drank of that spiritual rock that followed them; and the Rock was Christ."

Yet the Israelites turned against God. And what happened?

Paul ended by showing God's judgment. "Nor let us commit sexual immorality as some of them did, and in one day twenty-three thousand fell; nor let us tempt Christ, as some of them also tempted, and were destroyed by serpents; nor complain, as some of them also murmured, and were destroyed by the destroyer" (1 Cor. 10:8–11).

You may die if you continue to disobey God. But that doesn't mean you are going to hell.

God, through Paul's writing, told the Corinthian church what happened to Israel for the same reason He is telling us today: "Now all these things happened as examples, and they were written for our admonition, on whom the ends of the ages have come" (v. 11).

So carnality is craving the exact opposite of what God wants for us.

You may be protesting, "But it's tempting out there." You just feel you've got to have alcohol or sex. You say it has overtaken you. But 1 Corinthians 10:13 reminds you, you're not the first to face temptation, and God is faithful to help you escape it.

But you won't escape if you love the temptation more than God. Then death will result.

Finally, carnality results in loss of eternal rewards. You may lose your assurance of salvation. Or you may lose your eternal reward.

The Loss of Eternal Rewards

Many people have misconceptions about heaven. Many believe that everyone is equal, and there are no problems in heaven. Paul didn't seem to think so. He warned the Corinthian Christians: "Now if anyone builds on this foundation with gold, silver, precious stones, wood, hay, straw, each one's work will become clear; for the Day will declare it, because it will be revealed by fire; and the fire will test each one's work, of what sort it is. If anyone's work which he has built on it endures, he will receive a reward. If anyone's work is burned, he shall suffer loss; but he himself will be saved, yet so as through fire" (1 Cor. 3:12–15).

The word *fire* in the Bible means judgment. When applied to Christians, it means God's judgment or discipline in time and eternity. If you're living a faithful life, though not perfect, you will receive God's reward. Gold, silver, and precious stones aren't destroyed in fire. But if you're building your foundation on wood, hay, and stubble, your work will burn quickly. There are two tests of your works: Do you work according to the Bible, and do you live for God's glory?

People who do good things like build hospitals and feed the poor often do them for the wrong reasons. And those works will be burned. Even a good sermon that prompts many to accept Christ could be burned if the preacher desires to impress or glorify himself. You'll still get in heaven if you are truly saved but by the skin of your teeth.

All of these consequences result from living a carnal life. However, before you become discouraged, let me remind you, there is a cure for carnality, just as there is a cure for cancer.

THE CURE FOR THIS LIFE-THREATENING DISEASE

Christians in the clutches of carnality often expect to be able to *will* their way out of sinful behavior patterns. If this system worked, there wouldn't be so many jokes about unfilled New Year's resolutions. The truth is, neither good intentions nor positive thinking are capable of putting the flesh in its place.

Years ago mental institutions used an ingenious test to determine whether their residents were ready to be released. The supervisor plugged the drain of a sink in a utility room and turned on the water. As the floor became flooded, he locked the patient in the room, equipped with a mop and bucket and instructions to clean up the mess. Later, the supervisor returned to see how things were going. If the patient had neglected to turn off the faucet, he or she was clearly not ready to go home.

Too many Christians are frantically trying to use their own willpower to mop the sin out of their lives. They don't look for a way to stop the source of the sin. They will mop until the day they die, to no avail; none of us has the power to overcome our own carnality because in our flesh dwells no good thing (see Rom. 7:18). Only God has provided a means of shutting off the faucet once and for all, and for living a genuine Christian life. As we grow to understand it, we discover that it is not a question of what we choose to do, but of whom we choose to reflect or be like.

If you've got the cancer of carnality, then all you need is the cure of repentance. Don't get mad at God, the Doctor, or His staff, committed believers. Don't blame fellow patients for your disease. Don't ignore the cancer because it may spread to other areas of your life.

The Greek word for *repentance* is *metanoa,* which means to change your direction. You've got to reintroduce harmony with God into a mind that is filled with chaos. The only way to become spiritually healthy is by coming to the place of true repentance. The cancer of carnality is cured by three potent remedies.

1. Carnality is cured when Christians bring themselves around to repent of their sin. That's easy medicine. You don't need a doctor. You can take the pill of repentance on your own. This over-the-counter drug can be found in 1 John 1:9: "If we confess our sins, He is faithful [He won't be undependable] and just [He won't compromise His character] to forgive us our sins and to cleanse us from all unrighteousness."

In other words, you don't need chemotherapy if you take care of your carnality now. Just come clean.

If sin breaks harmony with God, it's important you confess immediately, not at the end of the day. He paid a high price for your sins—His only begotten Son. So your confession is like saying, "God, sprinkle the ever-present blood of Jesus on my sin." God cleanses us from all unrighteousness because we may not know something is a sin and may have even forgotten sins that have been committed. So confess the ones you know, and He will take care of the others.

How do you know it's a sin? One way is the Word of God. Another is a built-in sin detector called your conscience. If you walk through a metal detector with keys in your pocket, it will beep. If you walk through life with sin, the Holy Spirit who dwells in you will beep your conscience. Don't ignore the sound.

2. Carnality is cured when Christians bring their brothers or sisters to repentance. The carnal Corinthians had improved by the time Paul wrote to them in his second epistle. Why? Because he had confronted them. (Yes, they got mad. But they got over it.)

Another key passage is Galatians 6:1. "Brethren, if a man is overtaken in any trespass, you who are spiritual restore such a one in a spirit of gentleness, considering yourself lest you also be tempted."

The Greek word for *caught* means to be overtaken. In other words, you are stuck in the quicksand of sin. The Greek word for *restore* means to mend or put back together—not tear apart. So those who are spiritual aren't the ones who get on the phone and say, "Girl, girl, girl! Let me tell you what I just found out." You're just as carnal as the one you're talking about. James

5:19–20 reminds us that you save a brother from ruining his life—from death—if you go and restore him.

3. Carnality is cured when Satan's judgment brings the Christian to repentance. You can wreck the ship of your life into the rocks and reeves of carnality if you don't have the oars of faith and a good conscience. Then you can be delivered over to Satan, which means to be excommunicated by the church and turned over to a world that will beat you into coming back.

Paul entrusted Timothy, his young disciple, with the work of fighting God's battle for men's souls and admitted that some early Christians had had to be given over to Satan for punishment. He said, "This charge I commit to you, son Timothy, according to the prophecies previously made concerning you, that by them you may wage the good warfare, having faith and a good conscience, which some having rejected, concerning the faith have suffered shipwreck, of whom are Hymenaeus and Alexander, whom I delivered to Satan, that they may learn not to blaspheme" (1 Tim. 1:18–20).

And in his letter to the Corinthians Paul mentioned the man who had an incestuous relationship with his stepmother and committed him to the same fate: "Deliver such a one to Satan for the destruction of the flesh, that his spirit may be saved in the day of the Lord Jesus" (1 Cor. 5:5).

If a child won't listen to his parents, he's put out and eventually picked up by the police as a vagrant or runaway. If you're a child of God and you won't listen, He will kick you out of His house of protection and blessing and let Satan pick you up.

There have been times I've observed people riding an elevator in a skyscraper, from the basement to the top floor, struggling and straining to hold on to heavy luggage. And I think, *Why don't they put their bags down?*

It's the same question God must be asking you if you're carnal. By grace, He's saved you through Christ. You're on the elevator to heaven. So why carry the heavy load of willful sin through life when the weight of His grace will unload it? Or to say this in another way, why not unload the rats in the rear?

WHY NOT UNLOAD THE RATS IN THE REAR?

Handley Page, a pioneer in the world of aviation, was flying one of his finest planes across the Middle East long ago. Unbeknown to him, a large rat had crawled into the cargo area behind the cockpit before takeoff, attracted by the smell of food. While cruising several thousand feet in the air, Page heard the sickening sound of gnawing in his small plane. Realizing that he was not alone, his heart began to pound. Hydraulic lines and control cables ran throughout the cargo area. One misplaced bite could disable the aircraft and send him crashing to his death. There was no such thing as an autopilot at that time and being alone, Page could not abandon the controls to deal with his uninvited guest.

It was possible to land, but from his current altitude, there might not be time for him to descend safely before disaster struck. Besides, touching down on the uncertain desert sand was risky, and his chances of being able to take off again would have been more difficult.

Then Page recalled some information he once thought of as mere trivia: Rats require more oxygen to survive than humans and oxygen decreases as altitude increases.

Page pulled back on the yoke, causing the aircraft to climb higher and higher. Up, up, up he flew. In a few short moments, the gnawing stopped. A few hours later, when he was safely on the ground, Page discovered a dead rat lying just behind the cockpit.

Have you heard that gnawing sound before? If so, perhaps the "rat of sin" is at work nearby. He has a voracious appetite. And he spreads diseases like immorality, marital discord, and worldliness. Don't let him keep nibbling. Eventually, he will devour your devotion and send your faith crashing to the ground.

Instead, climb higher. Soar! The air might be a little thin if you are not used to flying so high. But keep going—the Spirit will keep you alert and awake.

Keep on climbing until the gnawing stops. Keep climbing until God brings victory where you did not think victory was possible. Keep climbing until Satan and the old life he dangles before you fall to the floor and die for lack of air.

Once you do, you will discover some breathing room you never knew about—all the space you need to be the new and improved you God created on Calvary. Remember you are with Him!

5

THE GOAL: THE ROAD TO SPIRITUAL MATURITY

AS CHAPLAIN FOR the NBA Dallas Mavericks, I lead a Bible study once a week before the games to encourage the guys in their spiritual lives. For my services, I receive six free tickets and a VIP parking pass so I can bring my family to the games. For one reason or another my family may be unable to attend so I will invite a few men from the church I pastor. I usually advise them to ride with me and take advantage of my free VIP parking pass; otherwise, they will each be charged five dollars for parking.

We enter the arena through a private entrance—the one that Michael Jordan, Isaiah Thomas, Kevin Johnson, Shaquille O'Neal, and all the other NBA stars go through. Since the men are with me, the guard at the door will let them through.

Once inside the arena, we use a private elevator that is for VIP use to get to the lower floor. Since the men are with me, they enter this elevator and go down to the lower level where there is a private VIP dining room. Since they are with me, the host allows them to enter this dining room. They are led to a table at which they are served a free, three-course meal.

As the National Anthem begins to play, signaling the start of the game, they do not have to go back to the main floor of the arena. Instead, since they are with me, they will wait for the Mavericks to exit the nearby locker room. They will then line up behind them and enter the court from a private underground tunnel. They will be so close to the team as they step onto the court, some might think they are on the payroll—and this privilege belongs to these men since they are with me.

They do not sit in the inexpensive seats, which are located high up in the nosebleed section. You see, my tickets are located courtside—midcourt to be exact. My friends sit so close to the action, they can almost touch the players as they pass. They enjoy the game from the best and most expensive seats in the house, at no charge to them, simply because they are with me.

Finally, the game ends, the crowd rushes out the exits to get to their automobiles. My friends need not rush, however, because they do not have to follow the crowd. They exit through the private tunnel and go back up the private elevator to the private entrance where they enter the private parking lot. They will be halfway home before most people have been able to exit the general parking lot, simply because they are with me.

My friends could not have enjoyed such an evening had they not been accompanied by the team chaplain.

They enjoy all the rights and privileges I enjoy for one reason and one reason alone: *They are with me!*

In the same way we have a new identity and enjoy all the privileges of our Lord Jesus Christ, simply because we are with Him. Listen to the words of the apostle Paul: "God, who is rich in mercy, because of His great love with which He loved us, even when we were dead in trespasses, made us alive together with Christ, (by grace you have been saved), and raised us up together, and made us sit together in the heavenly places in Christ Jesus, that in the ages to come He might show the exceeding riches of His grace in His kindness toward us in Christ Jesus" (Eph. 2:4–6).

Do you see that Jesus was saying *we are with Him*, which means that His position is our position, His authority is our authority, His rights and privileges are our rights and privileges. He is seated on the right hand of God in honor and power and we are seated right there with Him!

NOW THAT YOU'RE IN CHRIST, BE LIKE HIM

What would you say about a bird that would not fly? A lion that would not roar? A fish that would not swim? A rabbit that would not hop? You would have to conclude: These animals are not being true to their nature since birds fly, lions roar, fish swim, and bunnies hop.

However, if a lion did not know itself, it might try to hop. Or if a bird was confused about its nature, it might try to swim in the depths of the ocean. Likewise, a Christian who does not know who he is, will not live the victorious Christian life. One of the fundamental reasons for spiritual defeat is a poor understanding of our identification with Christ.

Take a look in the mirror. That person you see was cocrucified, coburied, and coresurrected with Christ. In the eyes of God, you died two thousand years ago when Jesus did. You lay in the tomb with Him. When He rose, you came along.

This process of identification reminds me of the jumper cables I keep in my car. One side hooks onto the good battery that holds the power, the other to the dead one. Once the connections are complete, the car with the dead battery can be started because the energy of the good battery flows through it. The dead battery becomes "alive" again, through no action of its own.

In the first century, the "Good Battery" died, then came back to life with all the power necessary to jumpstart those of us who are dead in sin. The cable of the Holy Spirit connects my dead spirit with Jesus' victory on the cross, as I mentioned in the last chapter.

The result: My spirit "turns over" and I am raised to walk in newness of life with Christ. Romans 6:4 explains that this identification occurs symbolically for us through baptism—an event that takes on far greater significance when you understand the meaning of the Greek word from which it is derived. To "baptize" literally means to plunge or dip, in the way one would plunge a piece of cloth into a vat to dye it. Any fabric "baptized" in a vat of purple dye became purple, its color absorbed from the dye. In the same way, the fabric of our being is saturated and permeated by the power of Jesus' life.

Let me make another analogy. As the pastor of a church, I have the privilege of performing marriage ceremonies. In every procedure I ask, "Who gives this woman to be married to this man?" The young lady's father (or someone else selected to take his place) steps up and says, "I do." Once he performs this task, he sits down with the guests. Papa's part of the ceremony is over. In fact, things grow worse for the poor man. Right after he recites his line, a young upstart walks up and takes his daughter's hand. Within ten minutes, I pronounce these two as one.

In order to sympathize with the father, we must understand what happened to the daughter: A transformation took place. She walked in the door as Miss Jones, his daughter, but she is walking out as Mrs. Smith, that upstart's wife! This change in identity will revolutionize the most important relationships in her life. Suddenly, the man who has spent the past eighteen-plus years raising her has been superseded by a relatively unknown young man. She now belongs to her husband, and is no longer "on the market" for suitors. To them she can now say, "Sorry. I am married."

This is an especially apt analogy, since the church is referred to in Scripture as the "bride of Christ." When we were joined with Him through spiritual baptism, we were transformed. No longer do we answer to the father of lies. It's time for us to move out of Satan's household altogether. We have now been joined with Jesus. He is the head of our new family, and we owe Him our faithfulness and loyalty.

When Satan rears his head and brings temptations our way—which he is certain to do—we flash our wedding ring of faith in his face and say, "Sorry. I'm married now. I have a brand new name and a new life to go with it. The person I was, along with all my old habits and shortcomings no longer exists."

A wedding ceremony generally takes place only once. However, we renew our wedding vows at the start of each new day, and again throughout the day as we face decisions which propose a compromise of our commitment to stay married to the same person. Living the Christian life is no different. Choosing to yield ourselves to God is a process—not an event—that will continue throughout our lives. Satan will see to it that we have no shortage of opportunities to bail out of our bond with Christ. When we are faced with decisions to yield or not to yield, our ability to stand firm will depend to a great degree on how fully we realize who we are in Christ.

NEW IDENTITY-NEW AUTHORITY

One of the great assertions regarding the Christian life was made by Paul when he said, *"I can do all things through Christ who strengthens me"* (Phil. 4:13). Wow! Paul's point is that along with his new identity in Christ comes new authority from Christ to experience all that Christ has provided.

If I had the fingers of Mozart, there would be no musical arrangement I could not play. If I possessed the mind of Einstein, there would be no mathematical formula I could not solve. If I had the legs of Michael Jordan, there would be no slam dunk I could not make. If I have the life of Christ within me, there is no spiritual victory I cannot experience.

And although I am not Mozart, Einstein, or Jordan, I do have the life of Christ within me as a Christian.

God has given me everything I need to be victorious; I just need to use it.

With our new identity comes new authority. We are with Him. We are complete in Christ.

WORKING OUT YOUR SALVATION

Does possessing this completeness of Christ automatically guarantee our experiencing this completeness? No! Spiritual growth is guaranteed, but it is not automatic. In his letter to the church at Philippi, Paul explained, "Therefore, my beloved, as you have always obeyed, not as in my presence only, but now much more in my absence, work out your own salvation with fear and trembling; for it is God who works in you both to will and do for His good pleasure" (2:12, 13).

Think of it; Paul was so assured of the completeness of Christ, he could confidently tell his readers they could experience the full outworking of their salvation even in his absence. How? By working out what God had already worked in. God expects us to grow spiritually, and we have an active part in that growth.

Let's look at spiritual growth: first, at some prevalent misconceptions; then, at the process of spiritual growth Peter outlined in 2 Peter 1.

Misconceptions about Spiritual Growth

Let's expose four prevalent misconceptions before moving on:

First, spiritual growth has to do with earning God's favor. Not so. Romans 5:8 tells us that while we were yet sinners, Christ died for us. God chose to love us unconditionally before we were saved, and He continues to do so now that we have yielded our lives to Him.

Obviously, we cannot earn what God gives us unconditionally. If we become mature believers, God will love us. If we do not, He will love us just as much. Spiritual growth is not a means of earning favor with God. As we will see, it is a matter of glorifying God, increasing our effectiveness as His witnesses, and enjoying the life He has given to us.

Second, spiritual growth has to do with knowledge. Do not forget that Jesus accused the Pharisees—the most learned theologians of His day—of spiritual bankruptcy. It is not enough to be able to quote Scripture verses. Maturity requires wisdom: the ability to successfully apply biblical knowledge to everyday living.

Third, spiritual growth has to do with church-related activities. Matthew 7:22, 23 makes it gravely clear that you can be absorbed by the things of God, yet **lost**: "Many will say to Me on that day, 'Lord, Lord, have we not prophesied in Your name, cast out demons in Your name, and done many wonders in Your name? And then I will declare to them, 'I never knew you; depart from Me, you who practice lawlessness.' "

Busy believers are not necessarily growing in the faith. Consider the church at Corinth, one of the largest and most active churches in the New Testament. It was chastised by Paul for carnality.

Maybe you've been a deacon for a decade or a teacher or a choir member. All are valid and important ministries. Spiritual growth, however, is a completely different issue.

Finally, spiritual growth has to do with prosperity. Some well-meaning preachers would have you believe this, but it is just not so. The Bible provides plenty of examples of poor Christians who are spiritually mature. In 2 Corinthians 8:1–5, for instance, we are told that the Macedonian churches had an abundance of joy and a deep commitment to give, despite persecution and poverty.

I have nothing against success. Praise God if He allows you to gain enough education and expertise to become a professional in your field and enjoy a measure of prosperity! Remember, Luke was a physician. God used this faithful follower of Christ to write two books of the Bible: Luke and Acts. Paul was among the most brilliant, well-educated men of his day. God used his intellect to spread the Gospel throughout much of the known world and to pen thirteen of the New Testament books, more than any other writer in the entire Bible.

Certainly, God can use your education and your professional expertise. Indeed, that is His desire. Your level of spiritual maturity, however, cannot be determined by your resume or your profit-and-loss statement.

Do not fall into the trap of concluding that affluence naturally follows spiritual growth. Satan amasses wealth too.

Now that we have corrected the misconceptions, let's look at the process of spiritual growth by going back to Peter's statement about spiritual growth.

Great and Precious Promises

After Peter said we have everything we need to live out our commitment to Christ, he went on to say God's divine power has given us "exceedingly great and precious promises, that through these you may be partakers of the divine nature, having escaped the corruption that is in the world through the lust" (2 Peter 1:4). Peter packed a great deal of theology into those few words. Let me summarize it this way. When you became a Christian, God placed His nature within you. Through the Holy Spirit, His character and His personality took up residence inside you.

While you still resided comfortably within your mother's womb, every characteristic of who you were to become was already locked within your DNA. Skin and eye color, hair color and texture, the number of fingers and toes—even tendencies toward certain temperaments and personality traits—all exist from the moment of conception. No one has to do anything to put them there; it is an automatic part of the process.

Upon your birth, those characteristics, once locked within your genes, began to manifest themselves outwardly. You didn't have to visit the parts department at the maternity ward and place an order for eyebrows or select some hair from among the choices in a catalog. Those things were part of your nature from the beginning.

As the baby's body grows, the pituitary gland, and other glands and organs, signal the body to provide what is needed for development. Humans do not need new programs to upgrade them, like computers. In God's wisdom, He saw fit to endow us with everything needed for our earthly existence in one serving!

The same is true spiritually. Once your spirit has been "fertilized" by the Spirit of God, you don't have to say, "Give me power." You already possess the power of the universe. You don't have to say, "Give me victory." You are already victorious. You don't have to say, "Give me faith." You already have more than enough to move mountains. You don't have to say, "Give me strength." You already have the might to withstand whatever comes your way. You needn't say, "Give me joy." You already possess the peace that passes all understanding.

This is a vital point. God's power and personality are in Christ, and Christ is in you. What more could you possibly need?

Of course, if this were the end of the story, this book and others like it would be unnecessary. You and I both know that we live in a constant state of tension between what we are in Christ and how we behave in the flesh. We know we have been given joy, yet we feel depressed. We know God has given us power, yet we feel helpless. We know God has assured us of victory, yet we lose battle after battle. We know God has promised us success, yet we sometimes feel like such a terrible failure. How do we account for the gap between who we are and what we experience?

For the answer, let's return to our childbirth analogy. Remember that every detail of how a newborn baby will look at age forty is already there, locked within his DNA—even though it is probably not apparent as he lies in his crib. Even so, a growth process turns that infant into a forty-year-old adult.

The baby must be properly nourished. He must be kept warm and safe. He must be inoculated against debilitating or life-threatening diseases. He must not be abused or otherwise mistreated by his parents or peers. Overlooking these steps increases the risk that he will not grow into the mature adult he was destined to become.

In other words, the child's genetic target is *guaranteed*, but it is not *automatic*. All that God wants you to become is "encoded" in Christ, encrypted within His divine nature. It is a guaranteed, foregone conclusion that you have within you the capability to attain spiritual victory and maturity. But, like the human growth process, it is not automatic.

Just as a baby needs milk, you will need nourishment befitting a newborn Christian. Newborn Christians do not feed on a diet of "the hypostatic union" or discussions on "the ontology of Jesus before His incarnation." New Christians must begin with spiritual milk. Parents would seriously jeopardize the welfare of their baby if they gave him a steak. In the same manner, one would jeopardize a new Christian by giving him fancy words and theological jargon before he is able to chew it.

The spiritual growth process is described in 2 Peter 1. There, Peter outlined seven steps toward seeing the divine nature unfold with you: Make every effort to add to your faith goodness; and to goodness, knowledge; and to knowledge, self-control; and to self-control, perseverance; and to perseverance, godliness; and to godliness, brotherly kindness; and to brotherly kindness, love (2 Peter 1:1–7 paraphrased).

Peter began by telling us to "make every effort."

"Make Every Effort." The Christian life in many respects is like riding a bicycle. Forward motion keeps you upright and traveling. If you cease to move forward, gravity takes over and you fall to the concrete sidewalk or road!

The goal of the Christian life is the same as riding a bicycle: to keep pedaling forward while you are learning to steer around obstacles and corners. The life of grace is all about movement. We were not saved to sit, soak, and sour.

To experience the victory in Christ, Peter says, make every effort. That means "go for it." Work hard. Don't be diverted. Make growth a focal point in your life. Don't expect it to occur automatically because it won't.

The degree to which you "make every effort" is the degree to which you will experience spiritual success. If you have a half-hearted prayer life, you are going to get half-hearted responses. If you have a half-hearted study life, you are going to have a half-hearted growth life. If you have a half-hearted fellowship life, you are going to receive only half-hearted support from your fellow believers.

In the midst of all this effort, you may be tempted to lose sight of grace. You may wonder if I'm describing some kind of salvation-by-works scheme. On the contrary! All the diligent effort in the universe could not produce growth apart from grace. It was God's grace that made it possible for you to receive Christ and for His nature to reside in you.

Your efforts do not replace God's grace; they simply enable what God has put within you to grow to fruition. A trip through the birth canal does not mitigate God's role in the miracle of creation. Instead, it is part of His prescribed plan for turning potential into reality.

Make no mistake. You are saved by grace for free. Growth, however, comes with a price tag. Salvation has nothing to do with works. Sanctification has everything to do with works.

Once Peter let us know spiritual growth would take some effort on our part, he outlined the process. He said, " add to your faith."

"Add to Your Faith." The Greek word which we translate "add" has an interesting meaning. It is the same root word from which we get the words *chorus* and *choreography*. Each suggests the idea of working together—one in song, the other in dance. But the Greek implies another nuance. It refers to the financier who puts up the money for staging, props, rehearsal halls, and the other expenses attendant to the performance of the chorus. These individuals provided the resources to enable the ensemble to practice and perform in the most professional way possible. Through continued usage, the term came to be associated with anyone who furnished the support necessary to allow another individual or group to accomplish their intended purpose.

Let's return to the context of our verse. Peter was telling us that it was time we came alongside and began to support what God was doing. "Add to your faith." In other words, stop working against God's grace. Stop opposing His program. Instead, start cooperating.

God wants to give us unbelievable victory, peace, power, and strength. Stop working against Him!

How do we do that?

We add the attributes Peter mentions here: goodness, knowledge, self-control, perseverance, godliness, brotherly kindness, and love. We will look at several of these attributes in this chapter and in part two, "Training: The Process of Spiritual Growth."

"Add Goodness." A synonym for *goodness* is *virtue*, or *excellence*. In Greek, the word suggests the concept of mastering something so that it fulfills its intended purpose. If you were to "add goodness" to a knife, you would hone it to razor sharpness because knives were intended to cut. "Adding goodness" to a horse might mean premium feed and regular exercise because horses are meant to run fast.

As Christians, we are trying to become Christlike. We are striving to become what God wants us to be. So, Peter tells us that to our faith, we are to add a commitment to becoming a master Christian.

Rising to the level of "master" in any arena does not occur by accident. Wood carvers, for instance, don't become masters by taking an occasional whack at a piece of lumber. Electricians don't become masters by fooling with power lines now and then. (Then they'd be more likely to become dead electricians!)

Many of us have failed to grow in our faith because we are content to remain novice Christians. Just "getting by" is plenty for many of us.

Being satisfied with mediocrity is an obvious path toward failure in most human pursuits; it is nothing less in the context of spiritual growth.

Add virtue to your faith. Become a master Christian and fulfill your intended purpose.

Then Peter said, "and to goodness, knowledge."

"Add Knowledge." As you can see, Peter was climbing a ladder of logic. First, you get saved through faith. To your faith, you add excellence (goodness). But you can't steer a course toward excellence without the proper information.

The Christian's source of knowledge is God's Word, the Bible, our spiritual "meat and milk." The Bible is the nourishment our spirits require for their growth and development. You cannot become a master Christian without the right kind of feeding. We will look at the Bible in chapter six, "The Playbook: The Authority of Scripture."

"And to knowledge, self-control," Peter wrote.

"Add Self-control." Once you have attained knowledge, you must transform information into action. As a well-known manufacturer of athletic shoes has suggested, "Just **do** it." Fulfilling that assignment requires self-control, a better word for which might be *discipline.*

The disciplined individual controls his passions instead of being controlled by them.

But what about the new Christian? Or the long-time believer who is only just now recognizing the importance of putting his or her passions in their place?

That's where the church comes in.

It is a generally accepted fact that babies don't raise themselves. They need care, supervision, and guidance in order to grow into mature adults.

Baby Christians are no different. They can't grow without help. Spiritual growth occurs within an environment of loving accountability—precisely the atmosphere that should exist within the local church. We will look carefully at the church and the role it plays in victorious Christian living in chapter eight, "The Complete Roster: The Importance of the Local Church."

That's the process in a nutshell (we will look at some of these attributes more completely in Part Two, as I mentioned). And the process has its rewards.

FRUIT: THE BENEFITS OF SPIRITUAL GROWTH

Make every effort, Peter says, to make these qualities of spiritual life your own. When you do, you enjoy the result promised in 2 Peter 1:8: "For if these things are yours and abound, you will be neither barren nor unfruitful in the knowledge of our Lord Jesus Christ."

The result of growth is fruitfulness. It is the natural result of living in light of who we are in Christ.

When you walk through an apple orchard, you naturally expect to see apples. If you see oranges instead, it is a safe assumption that you're not in an orchard at all, but an orange grove. I can say this with certainty because *it is the nature of fruit to reflect the character of the tree on which it grows.*

It is nothing less than the law of nature: Apple trees bear apples, orange trees yield oranges, grapevines generate grapes, and *Christians produce Christlikeness.*

Christians are to allow nothing to interfere with the consistent development of their spiritual lives for two very important reasons.

1. Our Growth Is the Only Means of Fulfilling Our Purpose: To Give Glory to God.

We are saved to give glory to God. That, folks, is the whole point!

First Peter makes this very clear: "You also, as living stones, are being built up a spiritual house, a holy priesthood, to offer up spiritual sacrifices acceptable to God through Jesus Christ" (1 Peter 2:5).

Why did God create you? For Himself. Period. You may say, "So why do I go to work?" For the glory of God. "So why do I raise a family?" For the glory of God. "So why do I exercise, or cook meals or build a business or do any of the things I do?" For the glory of God.

When we begin to see the connection between our everyday activities and God's glory, we have begun to understand the point of 1 Corinthians 10:31: "Whether you eat or drink or whatever you do, do all to the glory of God."

We should also be reminded of this truth every time we pray the familiar words of the Lord's Prayer: "Our Father in heaven, hallowed be *Your* name. *Your* kingdom come, *Your* will be done, on earth as it is in heaven" (Matt. 6:9,10).

If those first lines don't serve as a sufficient reminder, the closing line should certainly drive the point home: "For *Yours* is the kingdom and the power and the glory forever. Amen" (Matt. 6:13).

If we do all to the glory of God, does that make a difference to Him? Let's look again at the concept of God's glory so we can understand its various aspects. First, there is God's intrinsic glory. It is the manifestation of who He is. Nothing we can do will add to or subtract from that glory. In other words, God does not become more "Godlike" simply because we do Him the favor of growing spiritually. God's glory exists apart from anything we say or do.

Second, God has ascribed glory. We ascribe glory to God when we recognize His intrinsic glory. Even a sinner ascribes glory to God simply by saying, "What a beautiful day." Though unintentionally, he has acknowledged the beauty of God's creation.

Men and women do not have intrinsic glory. That's why our appearance and apparel mean so much to us. We're hoping for some ascribed glory, which will result in compliments. Still, nothing on the outside affects what we are like on the inside. Deep down inside, a king is nothing more than an ordinary person with a regal robe.

Some people spend inordinate amounts of money, which they often cannot afford, on luxury automobiles, simply for the sake of ascribed glory. After all, if you're driving down the avenue in a Mercedes Benz, you're likely to be treated with more respect than some poor guy in a battered Volkswagen. Appearance is everything. You look like something special in a big, fancy car—even if you may have to sleep in it at night.

For us, ascribed glory is an artificial additive to life. For God, it is a simple recognition of the fact that He is in complete control. The truth is, we cannot have beautiful days without God. Farmers cannot receive rain without God. We are nothing without God. "In Him we live and move and have our being" (Acts 17:28).

Do you know why we pray before eating? It's not just because we have heard the adage: "A prayer a day keeps the devil away." We pray before meals to ascribe glory. "Lord, I recognize that the food on this table is a result of your blessings, whether directly or indirectly."

The question, then, is not whether God deserves the glory we ascribe to Him. Instead, the issue is whether we will ascribe to Him the glory He deserves.

When we begin to realize that God's highest goal is to glorify Himself, we cannot help thinking in human terms: "Is God getting a little carried away with Himself? Whatever happened to humility?"

Humility is a human virtue that grows from an understanding of whom we aren't. This attitude results from a proper perception of the relationship between God the Creator, and man, His creation. There is nothing haughty or prideful about the God of the universe conducting Himself as the God of the universe.

Would you criticize me for decorating my house according to my own taste? Unless you pay my bills, such decisions are mine to make. You may like contemporary furniture. That's fine, for your house. But as long as we are in *my* house, you will see antique or early American furniture if that's more my style. To put it in spiritual terminology, my house is meant to reflect my "glory."

When you shop for a car, you look for the car you will enjoy driving. When you shop for clothes, you look for styles you will enjoy wearing. After all, if you're going to pay the amount on the pricetag, you have that right.

In the same way, God—who is not limited either by budget or ability—created the universe for His pleasure.

God has invited us to share that pleasure. Unfortunately, man has misunderstood the invitation. Imagine welcoming a guest into your house with the familiar phrase, "Make yourself at home." Taking you literally, your visitor moves all his worldly possessions into your house, sells your favorite pieces of furniture, and begins an aggressive remodeling program by demolishing several walls. You expected your houseguest to make himself comfortable—not to take over.

The Lord has graciously invited us to make ourselves at home in this world. Instead, man has decided to take over. This is the source of all our personal problems and social crises. Man has tried to claim ownership of something that is not his own and consequently has incurred the wrath of God.

The more we grow spiritually, the better we reflect the glory of God and the less we muddy the waters with our own short-sighted agendas. John the Baptist understood this concept clearly. When his faithful followers remarked that the crowds who used to follow him were now thronging around Jesus, John said, "A man can receive nothing unless it has been given him from heaven. You yourselves bear me witness, that I said, 'I am not the Christ,' but 'I have been sent before Him.' He who has the bride is the bridegroom; but the friend of the bridegroom, who stands and hears him, rejoices greatly because of the bridegroom's voice. Therefore this joy of mine is fulfilled. He must increase, but I must decrease" (John 3:27–30).

Here was a man who knew who he *was* and who he was not.

Our growth as Christians enables us to be more "reflective" of God's glory, and to more effectively focus His light on our dark, needy world. Imagine what we could do in the world if we really did reflect God's glory. The power we would have is partly seen by the power of giant reflecting telescopes. They work on a simple principle: An enormous curved mirror gathers light from faint, distant stars and it reflects on a small eyepiece. The reflecting power of the mirror enables astronomers to view the wonders of space, just as we could enable our world to truly see the wonders of God's glory.

The second fruit directly related to our new ability to communicate with God is stability in our lives.

2. We Become More Stable.

In James 1:5–8, we read, "If any of you lacks wisdom, let him ask of God, who gives to all men liberally and without reproach, and it will be given to him. But let him ask in faith with no doubting, for he who doubts is like a wave of the sea driven and tossed by the wind. For let not that man suppose that he will receive anything from the Lord; he is a double-minded man, unstable in all his ways."

There's a parallel passage in Ephesians 4:13–15, where Paul explains why God gave leadership to the Church: "Till we all come to the unity of the faith and the knowledge of the Son of God, to a perfect man, to the measure of the stature of the fullness of Christ; that we should no longer be children, tossed to and fro and carried about with every wind of doctrine, by the trickery of men, in the cunning craftiness of deceitful plotting, but, speaking the truth in love, may grow up in all things into Him who is the head—Christ."

Have you ever watched a young child try to make a decision? "Mommy, can I sleep with my teddy bear?" she calls from her bedroom.

Dutifully, you retrieve Teddy.

"Mommy, can I have my panda instead?"

You give the child the benefit of the doubt. She may have been thinking of the panda when she asked for the bear.

"Mommy, I want Winnie the Pooh."

All right, that's enough! You insist that she select one friend to sleep with.

"I choose Winnie. No, wait. Panda. Or Teddy . . . *Mommmmmy!*"

If you let them, kids can drive you crazy getting this and getting that. (After all, isn't that what Moms and Dads are for?!)

Obviously, children cannot make rational, complex decisions. They lack the maturity required to postpone their gratification, to understand the long-term consequences of short-term choices, and to weigh the moral and ethical implications of what may otherwise seem an obvious option. That's why they need grown-ups.

Unfortunately, adults too often have difficulties in those same areas—especially when they pertain to spiritual considerations. No matter how old we are, the Bible is clear: We are no longer to be children. Spiritual maturity is a must if we are to sift through the confusing assortment of alternatives life puts before us and reach sound, dependable decisions in areas like who to marry, how to resolve family conflicts, what job to take . . . and all the other matters of life.

HOW LONG DOES THE PROCESS TAKE?

A final question must be addressed: How long does it take to grow to spiritual maturity? Paul gave us a hint in his first epistle to the Corinthians. Many Corinthians had received the truth and accepted Christ as Savior after Paul's visit to Corinth in 50 A.D. The first letter to the Corinthians was written five years later, about 55 A.D. In the third chapter, he informed the Corinthians of his disappointment over their lack of spiritual progress, as I mentioned in chapter four. This leads me to conclude that any Christian has the potential of becoming a mature, consistently victorious Christian within a period of five years.

This, however, is not a set standard. As any parent knows, chronological age and maturity aren't necessarily equal. It is possible, and unfortunately common, to be a long-time Christian and a spiritual infant.

Almost any married woman will agree from personal experience: A man's age and level of maturity are not necessarily related to each other. During a stereotypical midlife crisis, men can become more like teenagers than adults! Age and maturity are very different realities and are not to be confused.

This leads to a simple, yet profound, conclusion. *Rate multiplied by time equals distance.* That is, the distance we go as Christians—the level of spiritual growth we attain—is determined by the amount of time we devote to spiritual matters (the rate we travel) and the number of years we have been Christians. Some Christians crawl spiritually; others jog; still others run. It is not unusual to see younger Christians who run in their Christian experience, thus outpacing older Christians who crawl.

Some months ago, I began lifting weights seriously. Every morning I get up at 5:00 and go to the nearby health club to work out. Growing muscles and becoming stronger is hard work. Each morning I pump, groan, and sweat as I push myself through the workout. At first, I hated to think about the process of body building. It was hard, back-breaking work, but when I looked at the increased flab, shortness of breath, and unhealthy weight gain, something needed to be done and quickly.

After a few months of lifting, I noticed something exciting. Muscles were beginning to replace fat; it took me longer to get tired and people were complimenting me on how good I was looking. All of a sudden, weight lifting was a necessity. The more I lifted, the stronger I became.

The same thing is true of spiritual growth if we are going to handle our strong enemies, the world, the flesh, and the devil. We need to pump spiritual iron to garrison the necessary strength to handle our adversaries and look good for the kingdom of God.

And just as we often need a physical checkup to see how well our exercise program is working, we need a periodic spiritual checkup.

A Spiritual Checkup

It is standard procedure for pediatricians to weigh and measure infants and toddlers during a checkup. The doctor carefully considers the child's growth and development since the last visit and compares the youngster's height and weight with the medical community's chart of "normality." A sluggish growth rate might be a sign of trouble and lack of growth is cause for genuine concern.

Why the concern? Because the newborn can never become all that it needs to become without growth. While new parents are excited about the births of their little ones, they are not satisfied unless they see their children develop into maturity.

Unfortunately, the growth of newborn Christians is not often assessed as carefully. Many of our churches are populated by spiritual infants who should have developed into mature believers long ago (like the Corinthian Christians). Yet pastors and lay leaders have allowed themselves to become tolerant of spiritual immaturity.

Have you ever wished you could be as spiritual as a Christian brother or sister you know? You can! You have the same identity in Christ as he or she has. If your friend appears to be progressing while you are regressing, it's because they are being who they are in Christ—and you are not.

Consider the appliances in your home. The toaster toasts, the can opener opens cans, the refrigerator refrigerates, and the microwave "waves." Each has a different form and function. Yet they are all configured to draw power from the same source. Electricity. Why can't we do the same? All who belong to Christ are tapped into the same unlimited Power Source, even though we look and act differently.

In Part Two, "Training: The Process of Spiritual Growth," we will look at the essential pieces of the process—Scripture, prayer, the local church, and the grace of giving.

The victorious Christian life is ours for the taking. It is time for us to look and act like victors. Why?! Because we are with Him.

Do you know what that means? It means when Satan seeks to destroy us, we're with Him. When friends seek to discourage us, we are with Him. When our enemies try to crucify us, we are with Him. When we are tempted, we are with Him. Let's never forget our identity in Christ. We are with Him!

PART TWO

TRAINING—THE PROCESS OF SPIRITUAL GROWTH

6

THE PLAYBOOK: THE AUTHORITY OF SCRIPTURE

WHEN MY BOYS were young, I purchased bikes for them at Christmas. On Christmas morning, my task was to assemble their new toys. When I opened the box, I reviewed the rather comprehensive instructions and immediately decided I could get the job done quicker by using my own wisdom and ingenuity. *After all*, I thought, *I have a doctorate so I'm certainly smart enough to figure out how to put together a kid's bike.*

Eight hours later, my wife came to the back door, looked at the bike, which only had the handle bars attached to the frame, and offered me some very valuable advice. "Honey, why don't you use the directions?" (Simple, yet profound!) The reality was that the bicycle maker knew more about bicycle assembly than I did, doctorate or no doctorate.

Many Christians are defeated because they insist on running their own lives rather than following the guidelines for living that God laid down in His Word. The Maker of life knows far more about living life than we could ever know, and He's not open to suggestions or advice. God has spoken, and He has not stuttered! If we are ever going to experience successful and victorious Christian living, we must realize that God operates in the command mode. Like the E. F. Hutton commercial, when He speaks, everyone else need simply be quiet, listen, and obey.

So let's look at the importance of God's authoritative, inerrant Word, and it's relationship to the victorious Christian life.

THE POWER OF THE PLAYBOOK

The Bible may be among the books on your shelf, but it is far more than just that. The writer of Hebrews described the Word of God as "living and powerful, and sharper than any two-edged sword, piercing even to the division of soul and spirit, and of joints and marrow, and is a discerner of the thoughts and intentions of the heart" (Heb. 4:12).

The Bible is a living sword that can cut its way to your insides and separate what lies there. The sorting process goes something like this: "This is soul, that is spirit. This is perverted thinking, that is pure thought. This activity is just selfish ambition in disguise, that intention has the good of the Kingdom at its core." So much for our secrets!

That Word is the outbreathing of the mind of God. Check out 2 Timothy 3:16, 17 if you doubt this: "All Scripture is given by inspiration of God, and is profitable for doctrine, for reproof, for correction, for instruction in righteousness, that the man of God may be complete, thoroughly equipped for every good work."

The word *inspired* literally means "breathed out." So, we're not dealing with an ordinary collection of words on a page. Instead, the Bible contains the written record of what God has given us regarding Himself. And there is no task to which God has called us, no situation in which He would place us, no question He would prompt us to ask, and no need with which He might challenge us, that is not addressed within the precious pages of Scripture. Scripture is literally the exhaling of God—and when God exhales, things happen. After all He spoke and the world came into existence!

It is intriguing to note that Paul, a New Testament apostle, wrote Timothy, a New Testament pastor of a New Testament church in the New Testament city of Ephesus, and told him that the Old Testament (since that's all Timothy had) was sufficient for every aspect of his ministry. Now if the Old Testament was sufficient for Timothy, how much more sufficient is Scripture for us who have free and unlimited access to the Old and New Testaments?

I've heard the Bible described as God's "owner's manual" for human beings. You must work for a living, so the Bible will teach you how to be God's kind of worker. You must remain married to the same husband or wife, so you'll learn how to be God's kind of mate. The Bible is a manual for life, but it is much more than just a manual, more than an assortment of diagrams and a few words of instruction. To be fully equipped to live the victorious Christian life we need a source of both authority and enablement—a perfect combination of direction, motivation, and energy.

My mother's favorite medicine was castor oil. I mean, she used castor oil to treat anything and everything. If I had a headache, she'd say, "Get the castor oil." If I had a stomach ache, she'd say, "Get the castor oil." If I had a backache, she'd say, "Get the castor oil." It was the all-sufficient remedy for my every disease and my every pain. By today's high-tech medical standards, that old-fashioned comprehensive approach would be viewed as passé, but somehow, that old-fashioned remedy really worked.

The Word of God is a lot like castor oil, because it has the unique old-fashioned ability to fix whatever ails you. That's why we're supposed to develop a craving for Scripture.

A Craving for Scripture

Are you ready to commit to a healthier diet by digesting the Word of God? Or is this desire dependent on your emotions?

The apostle Peter told Jewish believers who were struggling in the midst of persecution, "As newborn babes, desire the pure milk of the word, that you may grow thereby" (1 Peter 2:2).

Hunger is more than an emotion. Nothing, I mean nothing, will substitute for our desire for food. No matter how we feel, we have to eat. And the longer we go without food, the more desperate we become to find some.

Once we do find food, one feeding is never enough. Before long we will hunger again. That's why most of us have two meals a day, and many others have three. And some even press on to four, five, or more feedings a day, counting snacks. The idea of going without food for all but the shortest interval is unthinkable. That's why many believe that the root word of *diet* is *die*.

Do you have that same insatiable hunger for Scripture? Or are you living on a spiritual crash diet, depriving yourself of biblical nourishment for days, weeks, or even months at a time without giving it a second thought. No wonder many of us become spiritually anemic!

KNOWING THE PLAYBOOK INSURES SUCCESS

Imagine the Dallas Cowboys lining up to go for a first down. It's time for Troy Aikman, the quarterback, to call the play. But he didn't come to practice so he doesn't know all the current plays. What's he going to do?

That's the situation we're in when we haven't read our playbook, the Bible, carefully. However, every Christian automatically receives two benefits when he studies the playbook.

1. You Know the Plays Because You Have Renewed Your Mind.

A renewed mind is something that the Bible guarantees, but not without the cooperation of the saint. Peter told the early Christians, "Grow in the grace and knowledge of our Lord and Savior Jesus Christ" (2 Peter 3:18).

When the Bible speaks of knowledge, it refers to understanding God and His ways through an intense study of His Word. Scripture provides this knowledge for us primarily in two ways. First of all, the Bible can teach us about God and how He relates to man through real-life episodes. (Soap operas really don't have anything on the Bible; you'll find sinners there too.) Often we can see parallels with situations in our own lives and act accordingly. For example, the book of Jonah demonstrates how God is patient with us and how He loves to show grace and mercy to us. The Ninevites were certainly deserving of punishment. They were known for their extreme brutality when they conquered other cities. Yet God gave them the opportunity to repent. This story proves that God is not a God who watches over us with a giant fly swatter, waiting to swat us whenever we make the slightest error.

The same Bible also teaches us that God hates sin. The epic journey of the children of Israel illustrates this point. God provided everything that the Israelites needed. When they were oppressed by the Egyptian army, God parted the sea. When they had nothing to drink but bitter water, God made the water sweet. When they were hungry, God gave them Kentucky Fried Chicken and rolls from heaven (quail and manna). No matter what they needed, God was quick to supply.

Yet God's patience grew thin with the Israelites. Time after time, they grumbled and disobeyed His instructions. Finally, God grew weary of their willful ignorance of His statutes and the wilderness became a permanent residence for a whole generation of people. No one—but no one!—is able to receive God's grace and play Him for a fool. We cannot live our lives thinking that we can pull the rug over God's eyes. In the first place, we do not have enough wool. Secondly, He could see through it anyway.

The Old Testament is rich with a plethora of stories able to help us understand how God deals with humanity. But this great treasury of truth is of no use to you if you do not access it by reading the Word. Dusty Bibles means dirty lives.

The New Testament is filled with propositional truths in the form of the apostles' letters, written to saints in centuries past. Many of the same dilemmas that beset the early church also attack us, as I mentioned in chapter one. These problems range from heresy to marital difficulties. Although the Scriptures do not provide an exact replica of every problem that can occur in life, they are more than adequate to provide us with the knowledge and skill for handling anything that may come our way. That's why much of this book is based on the writing of the early apostles, like Paul and Peter.

Having the right things in your mind will not automatically guarantee that you will follow them. But one thing is for sure. You will not do what is right if you are not aware of what is right. Any football player can run into the end zone, but only the one with the ball is capable of scoring.

Secondly, Scripture can be used to defeat the devil.

2. The Playbook Can Be Used to Defeat the Devil.

Far too often, Christians use Scripture against one another, rather than against the one who really needs to hear it, the devil! Jesus made this point inextricably clear during His confrontation with the devil in Matthew 4.

It is interesting to note, first of all, that "Jesus was led up by the Spirit into the wilderness to be tempted by the devil" (v. 1). Therefore, it was God's idea that Jesus take the offensive and meet Satan on his territory.

When you have God's Word by your side, you are ready to get it on with the devil, even on his turf. Without it, you're in trouble. Satan attacked Jesus at His point of need, hunger. He offered Jesus a solution to His hunger: turn stone into bread (v. 3). Jesus' response, however, was to quote Scripture.

Now this is very important. If the Living Word felt He needed to use the written Word (which He wrote) to deal with Satan, then how much more do you and I need to use that same Word to overcome the evil one. *One of the primary reasons you learn the Word is so that you can have Bible studies with the devil!*

Satan can handle you, but he can't handle God's Word. Jesus responded, "Man shall not live by bread alone, but by every word that proceeds from the mouth of God" (v. 4). Jesus was not saying, "Read a verse a day to keep the devil away." Rather He quoted Deuteronomy 8:3, Moses' record of God's supernatural provisions of manna for Israel in the wilderness. Jesus was saying, "Men live by two things not one: physical food and spiritual food."

As long as Satan is meeting the need, no matter how legitimate the need (food, shelter) the process is invalid. Men only live if God is the supplier. Far too many Christians are letting Satan and his surrogates meet the needs of their lives. And then they lose the victorious life.

Next, Satan took Jesus to the pinnacle of the temple and told Him to jump. Satan validated his request by quoting Scripture to Jesus: "For it is written, 'He shall give His angels charge over you,' and 'In their hands they shall bear you up, lest you dash your foot against a stone' " (vv. 6, 7).

Jesus responded with a very important phrase: *"On the other hand."* This invalidated Satan's use of Scripture. Jesus told Satan, "If you are going to use Scripture, use all of it and not only the part that suits your fancy and frees you up to justify your actions."

We'd do well to heed Jesus' advice. Scripture must be compared with Scripture so that we get what Paul Harvey calls, "the rest of the story." Jesus informed the devil that you don't tempt God or force Him into a corner so that He has to perform a miracle (a supernatural rescue by angels so Jesus' Messianic claim would be validated as the Jews saw Him descend from the top of the temple into the courtyard without being harmed).

"God will get His recognition His way and in His time," Jesus told the devil, "without your assistance, thank you very much!" There would be no compromise just because Satan could get it done quicker. No shortcuts to victory.

Finally, Satan took Jesus and showed Him all the kingdoms of the world and their glory and offered them to Him if He would only bow down and worship him (vv. 8–40). Of course, this was the devil's goal all the time.

Jesus responded, "Begone! God alone is to be worshipped and served." Again, Jesus quoted Scripture and after this third occasion, Satan left.

There is an important lesson to be learned at this point: Satan can't handle the use of Scripture against him more than three times, regarding any specific issue. God must like baseball; He tells Satan, "Three strikes and you're out!"

So how did the Son of God manage to maintain His resistance? By quoting Scripture.

"Jesus, you look hungry," the devil observed. "How about turning some stones into bread?" The answer: *"It is written."*

"Jesus, let me help You get recognition and acceptance and even bypass the cross." Again the response, *"It is written."*

"Jesus, what do You say about ruling the whole world? Just worship me." And the Lord replied, *"It is written."*

Of all the responses Jesus could have chosen, He elected to use Scripture to chop Satan into little pieces.

When it comes to the Word, Satan is a lot like Dracula. You remember those "B" movies, don't you? Each night, old Dracula would roam the woods, sucking the lifeblood out of one aspiring starlet after another. Finally, someone would remember the prescription for dealing with vampires. He would fashion a cross out of two pieces of wood. When the Count approached, the hero would hold that cross up in his face, rendering him powerless and vulnerable.

The Word of God has much the same effect on Satan. When is the last time you had a Bible study with the devil? In order to do that, you better prepare yourself by reading the playbook.

CONSULTING THE PLAYBOOK
DAY AFTER DAY

The writer of Psalm 1 suggested that we meditate on God's Word day and night. Was he suggesting that we seclude ourselves with our Bibles twenty-four hours a day? Of course not. Meditation, in this context, is a round-the-clock awareness of God's principles and His presence in our lives.

Bible study is a key part of that, whether it consists of five minutes of intense study, thirty minutes of casual reading, or listening to a recorded sermon or a radio broadcast as we drive to and from work. God's law is bouncing around in our brain at all times, shaping our consciousness and molding our behavior. In this way the Word of God is "sitting in judgment" over all of our lives all the time.

The meditation Psalm 1 talks about is an act similar to that of a cow chewing its cud. We have all observed a cow's mouth continuously moving around and around. When the cow gets tired, it will swallow the cud. When it desires to chew again, it will retrieve the cud from its stomach by regurgitating it back up into its mouth. This process will continue until the cud has been so completely dissolved it penetrates the cow's whole body.

This is precisely what God wants believers to do with His Word. He wants us to chew on it regularly, being prepared to regurgitate it when needed, until we have chewed it so much we don't have to regurgitate it because it has infiltrated our spiritual system. Then our actions and reactions will reflect His divine perspective.

Those who fail to meditate on Scripture will automatically begin to drive in spiritual reverse. They will be following the advice of the ungodly rather than the godly, as verse 1 of this psalm notes—and they will not be blessed.

The tragedy these days is that people want to come to church without letting the Word sit in judgment of them. They want license to pursue their secular desires without giving up the warmth and security of life in the family of God. Unfortunately, the rules of physics prevent us from being in two places at once.

The person who meditates on the Word will not face such a choice. The psalm says, "He shall be like a tree planted by the rivers of water, that brings forth its fruit in its season, whose leaf also shall not wither; and whatever he does shall prosper" (v. 2, 3).

This translates not only into a deep sense of well-being, but into a fail-safe system of productivity. If you're on the ragged edge of giving in to some sin, your awareness of God and His Word will stand like a guard rail before you. In order to get to the sin, you'll have to climb over God and His Word.

A Daily Habit

It's impossible to implement the Word without first becoming acquainted with it. You should begin by setting aside time each day to spend with your Bible. Many prefer early mornings, others choose the late evenings after the kids have gone to bed. The hour you select is not especially important. What counts is that you have made an appointment with God.

You should honor that commitment accordingly. Anything you allow to compete with your time with the Lord has the potential of stifling or stopping your spiritual growth. No wonder Satan works overtime to offer an abundance of available excuses. Perhaps it's the television or the telephone. Even a good book can be a diversion from the Good Book. It's up to you to clear these obstacles out of the way.

If you're having trouble identifying your highest priority, simply ask yourself, "What occupies the biggest piece of my time? Bible study? Television? Sports?" I'm not trying to point an accusing finger or set down any hard and fast rules about the length of your personal time with the Lord. However, consistent study is a vital discipline. Commit to a plan that works for you; then stick with it.

One suggestion I'd like to make is read through the Bible each year. Granted, not every part of the Bible is as exciting as others; for example, the genealogies may seem less than electrifying at first. But as you study those lists of people, you'll discover that God wasn't just name dropping. The genealogies in Matthew and Luke show that each person was a link in the lineage of Christ, proving that Jesus was who He said He was. Sometimes you may stumble across a verse that seems to have no relevance to you, only to find that it relates perfectly to an experience that occurs later in the day.

The truth is, studying the Word is sometimes like eating vegetables. They don't do a thing for your taste buds, but they'll work wonders in your bloodstream. Most of the stuff that tickles your taste buds is junk food, making you smile while you eat it and later disturbing your digestive system and clogging your arteries.

Besides your daily appointment with God, you should set aside regular times in your week for in-depth study of the Word. Your daily devotions help you see God's "big picture." Serious Bible study brings out the finer details.

As you study, *you should be looking for the new lesson God wants to teach you about Himself.* There is *always* a new lesson, because God is infinite and inexhaustible. That's why, after 100 million years in heaven, we'll feel like we're still just getting acquainted with Him. Like

God Himself, the Scripture is a well that never runs dry.

As we learn those lessons, *our next goal should be to consider what we should do differently.* Stopping short of this step turns our study into a waste of time. The apostle Paul told the Colossian Christians, "Let the word of Christ dwell in you richly" (Col. 3:16).

To dwell simply means to be at home. "Let the Word of Christ make itself at home in your life," Paul advised the early Christians. Now, if I came to your home and you said to me, "Evans, make yourself at home," I would strongly suspect that you were simply quoting a cliché. You really didn't mean that I should make myself at home.

What you really meant to say was, "Make yourself comfortable in *this room*, since it's the only one in the house that's clean. Don't look behind any closed doors. Don't poke around in the closets. In fact, stay right there in that chair and mind your own business while you're in my house. But, whatever you do, don't make yourself at home!"

How many of the doors in our lives have we closed in an effort to keep God out? Or how many times have we refused to live God's way or talk about His principles? Let's get serious! As we've already made clear, there are no secrets where God is concerned. He's not going to sit in that chair and mind His own business.

James compared the relationship between reading God's Word and living it to a man checking himself out in a mirror. He began by instructing the early Christians, "Be doers of the word, and not hearers only, deceiving yourselves." Then, he said, "For if anyone is a hearer of the word and not a doer, he is like a man observing his natural face in a mirror; for he observes himself, goes away, and immediately forgets what kind of man he was" (James 1:22–24).

Now, most women can't understand this analogy. When a woman walks past a mirror, she looks and looks and looks. Eventually, she walks away, then turns to look one more time in case she overlooked something. A man generally doesn't do that. He'll take a quick glance, conclude that everything is okay, then he's gone—without even noticing the gravy stain on his tie!

Better to take a long, lingering look at the Word, James advised. You'll spot those embarrassing stains right away and know just how to remove them. Then, you'll be equipped and enabled to put the Word to work and become an effectual doer, resulting in movement another mile down the road toward spiritual maturity.

James promised our Christian ancestors, "But he who looks in to the perfect law of liberty, and continues in it, and is not a forgetful hearer but a doer of the work, this one will be blessed in what he does." He shall be a victorious Christian.

THE PLAYBOOK CAN BE SUFFICIENT

When Christ was tempted in the wilderness, the angels did not come and minister to Jesus until after Satan left. I've always wondered, *Why would the angels come after the conflict was over?* The answer, I believe, is sometimes God leaves us alone with only His Word. Sometimes there seems to be little support, little encouragement, no friends—only God's Word. The question during these times is, "Is God's Word sufficient?" The answer, "Oh yes, it is!"

Suppose someone knocked on your door late at night. Upon opening your door, you discover a seven-foot, ten-inch giant of a man standing before you. He forces himself into your home and begins to take over the running of your house. Your whole family is terrified as he now occupies every room and controls your existence.

All of a sudden you remember 911. If you can only get the phone off the hook and dial 911, you can get help. You do so and a police car is sent to your home. Two policemen get out with the firepower around their waists to challenge your unwelcome guest. But the strong man fights back. That's when the two policemen use their walkie talkies to call for reinforcements. All of a sudden, twenty cars show up, more than enough help to rid you or your unwanted guest. You experience victory because of 911!

All Christians possess a 911 number thay can dial when Satan intrudes upon their lives, seeking to bring them to defeat. Our 911 number is, "it is written." When we dial that number the dispatcher, called the Holy Spirit, delivers our emergency plea for help to the Throne Room of God. He responds by sending whatever help is needed to remove the strong man from our lives and give us victory. So, when you are under spiritual attack, don't forget to dial 911. Satan can handle you, but he can't handle the Word of God. Remember, *"It is written."*

God has spoken and He has not stuttered!

You can advance your development in the faith by associating with someone who is advanced in the faith. In order to grow your renewed mind to maturity, both the Scripture and fellow Christians are a necessity. Paul was advanced in the faith much more so than was

Timothy. But it was the fatherly nurturing of Timothy that brought him to maturity. Paul wrote 1 and 2 Timothy to encourage Timothy to have moral courage. Timothy was to have confidence in the things Paul taught him and was to apply them even in stressful circumstances. Apparently, Paul's instruction took root in Timothy's life. Timothy grew up to be spiritually mature much as Paul. Hebrews 13:23 informs us that Timothy was imprisoned, most likely because of his convictions, just like his spiritual father, Paul.

The Sword of the Spirit

The sword is the only offensive weapon listed in our arsenal of faith; all others are designed for defense. The reason it is the only weapon listed is because it is all you need.

The sword of the Spirit is God's Word. It takes God's Word to turn our defense against Satan into a full-scale counterattack.

The Greek word used for *word* refers to the Word of God spoken as opposed to the written Word. Thus, the emphasis here is the actual use of Scripture in the midst of conflict. It means taking the sword out of the sheath and using it. Studying the Bible is critical, but it is not enough. Memorizing Scripture is crucial, but it is not enough. Meditating on Scripture is wonderful, but it is only using Scripture that matters. It means identifying the appropriate passages for the various conflicts you face and bringing those truths to bear on the situation. Martin Luther said it best: "The Bible is like a lion. You don't have to defend it; just let it loose. It will defend itself."

7

SIGNALS FROM THE COACH: THE POWER OF PRAYER

I HEARD A story once about a man who had always wanted to go on an ocean cruise. For years, he put away a portion of his meager earnings and finally saved enough to pay the fare: $1,300—every penny he had. In fact, he packed himself a basket full of peanut butter sandwiches because he knew he would not be able to spend another penny once he boarded the ship. As he enjoyed the swimming and the sun deck and the fresh air, he noticed how well the other passengers were eating. They seemed to do little else. Wherever he looked were lavish spreads of appetizers, salads, fruits, breads, and desserts. At the end of the long buffet tables chefs were carving mouth-watering slabs of beef, roast turkey, and rack of lamb. On the last day of the cruise, his curiosity got the better of him. He stopped a passing steward, who was carrying a particularly delicious looking room service tray.

"Excuse me, young man," he asked. "How much does a meal like that cost?"

The steward was taken aback by such a question, but managed an answer. "Sir, you don't understand. All the food you want is included in the price of your ticket."

How tragic to be given such a privilege and not use it.

As Christians, we share a common destination. Along the way, however, some of us eat better than others. We can feast our way through this life, dining lavishly on the grace of God. Or we can settle for a peanut butter sandwich. It depends on to what degree we access God's grace. The difference is prayer.

THE PRIVILEGE OF PRAYER

If we were to take a survey of married couples, we'd almost certainly find that one key distinction that separated the strong marriages from the stagnant ones is good communication. It's just about impossible to grow close to someone without clear, honest, two-way communication. Nowhere is that more true than in our relationship with God.

Certainly, God speaks to us through His Word. Certainly, we respond to Him through our obedience. But in His grace, He has given us access to His presence through prayer.

Prayer may be defined as regular communication with God in which committed believers develop an intimate fellowship with their Father. Unfortunately, many of us know our prayers so well, we need not think; the same old words automatically roll off our tongues.

The fact of the matter is the depth of our prayer life reflects the depth of our relationship with God. Anemic prayer reflects anemic spirituality. Conversely, growth in our prayer life equals growth in our spiritual life. This is why prayer was so intrinsic to the life of Christ.

Mark 1:35 records the busiest day in the earthly life of Christ, a day He preached in many synagogues. Yet on that day He did not sleep in to get more energy; instead, He rose before daylight to pray. The busier His schedule, the greater His need for God. When He was on His way to the cross He prayed in the Garden of Gethsemane. When He was suffering on the cross, He prayed.

Most of us have checking accounts at our local banks. Our checks give us the power and authority to make withdrawals from the bank, based on the amount of money in our accounts. When we write a check, the bank stands behind the endorsed check and releases that amount.

God has deposited the riches and righteousness of Christ Jesus, which Paul called "every spiritual blessing" (Eph. 1:3), into the spiritual bank account of every believer, as I mentioned earlier. The amount in the account is nothing short of staggering. Yet Christians seem unable to write spiritual checks against their account. The check writing process for Christians is called *prayer*.

The author of Hebrews summarized this unique privilege when he wrote, "Seeing then that we have a great High Priest who has passed through the heavens, Jesus the Son of God, let us hold fast our confession. For we do not have a high priest who cannot sympathize with our weaknesses, but was in all points tempted as we are, yet without sin. Let us therefore come boldly to the throne of grace, that we may obtain mercy and find grace to help in time of need" (Heb. 4:14–16). Jesus Christ, our Savior, is also our sympathetic High Priest who gives us an open invitation to approach God for help in time of need.

God has set aside a place where we can come and freely receive His mercy. It's called the "throne of grace," a phrase which could rightly be transliterated "the throne that dispenses grace." What a rich privilege to be invited into that holy place—and to be told to approach with confidence.

If you go to Washington, D.C., you can take a tour of the White House. You'll be escorted through various rooms by a tour guide, while being watched carefully by surveillance cameras and Secret Service agents. Certain rooms will be off-limits, however. They are private areas reserved for the president and his family, various staff members, and visiting dignitaries.

Some time ago, I was invited to the White House to confer with President Bush. The visiting tourists who were there that day could not come with me; they weren't there by the president's invitation. But when I went up to the guards and presented my letter and credentials, they escorted me right into the oval office.

Any human being can walk the grounds of God's world and enjoy the benefits of sunshine, fertile ground, refreshing water, and so on. But, through Christ, God has issued a personalized invitation to each and every one of us who names the name of Christ to come boldly into a very private room, the throne room of grace.

PRAYERS THAT PASS THE CEILING

Sometimes, Christians march boldly into the throne room, and then they haven't got a clue what to say. It's like the youngest child at a family meeting. The little one waves his arm to get attention for many minutes. Then when he is the center of attention, he forgets what he wanted to say.

Or Christians lay their requests at God's feet, then get no response to their prayers. That's like turning around to discover you were carrying on a "conversation" with someone who left the room when you weren't looking. There you are, thinking that a dialogue was taking place when, in reality, you were simply wasting your breath.

Too many Christians have all but given up on prayer, feeling that the Lord either isn't listening or isn't inclined to respond. It seems as though the words of the old cliché, "Their prayers are bouncing off the ceiling" are true.

What does it take to get our prayers *past* the ceiling?

I would suggest that we start with some proper instruction in the art of prayer. Fortunately, just such a lesson appears in Matthew 6:5–15. The teacher is Jesus Himself. He left an example we call The Lord's Prayer:

> Our Father in heaven,
> Hallowed be Your name.
> Your kingdom come.
> Your will be done
> On earth as it is in heaven.
> Give us this day our daily bread.
> And forgive us our debts
> As we forgive our debtors.

> And do not lead us into temptation.
> But deliver us from the evil one.

Every one of us has recited the familiar words of the Lord's Prayer a hundred times. Perhaps you learned it in your Sunday School class as a child. Maybe you repeated the words each night at bedtime as your mother or father looked on. If you were involved in sports during high school, your team might have nodded at God by reciting these words after practices or before games.

Granted, the words themselves are deeply meaningful, but they weren't meant to be treated like some magical incantation or meaningless tradition. Jesus prefaced His petition by saying, "This is *how* you should pray." He did not say, "This is *what* you should pray." The specific words are not as important as the principles behind them.

Principle One: The Lord Is Interested in Humility, Not Stage Presence

You can't appreciate the Lord's Prayer until you look at the prayers of the hypocrites and pagans. For that insight, we look at what Jesus said before He repeated the Lord's Prayer. He told the disciples, "When you pray, you shall not be like the hypocrites. For they love to pray standing in the synagogues and on corners of streets that they may be seen be men. Assuredly, I say to you, they have their reward. But you, when you pray, go into your room, and when you have shut the door, pray to your Fahter, who is in the secret place; and your Father who sees in secret, will reward you openly" (Matt. 6:5, 6).

No doubt you've heard people who can mesmerize entire congregations with their litany of linguistics. Maybe you've even said to yourself, "I wish I could pray like he can pray!" According to this verse, that wish might be unwise. Eloquence impresses people, not God. The Lord is interested in humility and sincerity, not stage presence.

One evening at bedtime, a little boy prayed loudly from his room, "Lord, bless Mommy and Daddy. And, Lord, give me a new bicycle!" His mother came in, holding her ears, and said, "Son, you don't have to shout. God can hear." He answered "Yes, Mommy, but Grandmother can't. She's clear down the hall!" Prayer has nothing to do with style or flair. I can recall a man in our church who had trouble putting two words together without stumbling—especially in prayer. Though he did his best, his constant stammering, lost trains of thought, and mangled English began annoying other members.

Eventually, some people in the church confronted him. "We don't like the way you pray," they complained.

His response to their complaint was simple and direct. "I was not talking to you."

Don't let your prayers degenerate into a performance for your family or friends or fellow Christians—or your grandmother! Your goal is neither to impress nor inform other people. Instead, find a place to be alone with God. (Parents, be creative!) Private prayer should be an intimate encounter between Creator and creation.

Jesus went on to tell His disciples, "And when you pray, do not use vain repetitions as the heathen do. For they think that they will be heard for their many words. Therefore, do not be like them. For your Father knows the things you have need of before you ask Him" (Matt. 6:7, 8).

Meaningless words do not translate into meaningful prayer. There's nothing wrong with teaching a child to pray, "Now I lay me down to sleep," and so on. But if that's as far as you've gotten after twenty or thirty years of praying, that's meaningless repetition. If you recite the same worn out phrases before a meal and call it grace, you may have *quoted* a ditty, but you have not *prayed.*

After Jesus shocked His audience with these examples of what prayer is not, He offered an example of the real thing, packed with profound theological truth. For the next principles let's look at the words of the Lord's Prayer.

Principle Two: His Names Describe Who He Is (Our Father)

Jesus started out, "Our Father in heaven." Right off the bat, He answered the question, Who can pray? The Lord's Prayer is intended for *believers*, because only through Christ do we become sons and daughters who can legitimately call God, "Father."

This may come as bad news to baseball and football teams and to anyone else who treats the Lord's Prayer as a good-luck charm. Still, the fact remains that prayer is a part of the familial relationship that exists between God and His children. It is within this context that we call God "Abba Father" or "Daddy."

At the same time, we must remember that we serve an awesome God, an all-powerful *heavenly* Father, the Creator of the universe. Familiarity must never give way to disrespect. We maintain this balanced perspective by giving God the honor and praise He deserves in the next words of Jesus' prayer: "Hallowed be Your name." The word *hallowed* means to sanctify or to set apart, to deem as special.

In biblical times names reflected character. So, if you could understand a person's name, you came closer to understanding the person. Let's look at some of God's names in the Old Testament to see if He's a person to go to when we need help.

We have heard God called *Elohim*, the Creator God. He is *Adonai*, the Lord. We know him as *Jehovah*, the God who keeps His covenant. Here are some others:

- *El Elyon:* "The Most High God."
  El Elyon describes the God who sits in heaven, looks down and says, "Everything is in My hand." When you call on *El Elyon*, it is a way of saying that no matter what's going on, everything is under His control.
- *El Olam:* "The Everlasting, Unchanging God."
  No matter how volatile your circumstances, no matter how unstable your life may seem, you serve a God who is the same for all time.
- *El Shaddai:* "God Almighty, full of grace."
  When I need what I don't deserve, *El Shaddai* is there to make up the difference with His grace.
- *El Roi:* "The God who sees."
  When I'm hurting, I need *El Roi*, for God is so intimately connected with my circumstances that He hurts with me.
- *Jehovah Raah:* "The Lord, my Shepherd."
  When I don't know which direction to take in life and I get down on my knees and call on *Jehovah*

Raah, I know that this sheep is about to be aimed in the perfect direction.

- *Jehovah Sabbaoth*: "The Lord of Hosts."
  When I find myself in a whole lot of trouble and nobody seems ready to come to my aid, I remember *Jehovah Sabbaoth*. If necessary, He will send all the angels of heaven to get me where I need to go.
- *Jehovah Jireh*: "The Lord will provide."
- *Jehovah Rapha*: "The Lord who heals you."
- *Jehovah Shalom*: "The Lord, my peace."
- *Jehovah Shammah*: "The Lord who is always near."

Lest you think we've slipped into the pit of pantheism, make no mistake—there is only one God. These names only describe parts of our multifaceted Father in heaven. Hallowed be His name.

We have seen that successful prayer requires an understanding of the person of God. But we must also align ourselves with His program, as the next words, "Your kingdom come, Your will be done on earth as it is in heaven," suggest.

Principle Three: We Must Align Ourselves with His Program (His Will)

God's kingdom cannot be found on any map. Rand-McNally can't draw a line around it because it does not primarily have to do with geography. The Kingdom of God exists wherever His divine rule is acknowledged.

To understand the phrase "Your will be done" we must take a trip to heaven and see just *how* God's will is done. The prophet Isaiah gave us a bird's-eye view:

In the year that King Uzziah died, I saw the Lord sitting on a throne, high and lifted up, and the train of His robe filled the temple. Above it stood seraphim; each one had six wings: with two he covered his face, with two he covered his feet, and with two he flew. And one cried to another and said:

> "Holy, holy, holy, is the LORD of hosts;
> The whole earth is full of His glory!"

And the posts of the door were shaken by the voice of him who cried out, and the house was filled with smoke.
Then I said:

> "Woe is me, for I am undone!
> Because I am a man of unclean lips,
> And I dwell in the midst of a people of
>   unclean lips;
> For my eyes have seen the King,
> The LORD of Hosts."

Then one of the seraphim flew to me, having in his hand a live coal which he had taken with the tongs from the altar (Isa. 6:1–7).

Notice that the angels do God's bidding *without question.* No debate, no discussion, no delay. Satan, the last inhabitant of heaven who followed a different agenda, doesn't live there any more. In heaven, the angels respond to God's commands *readily, eagerly, fervently, and constantly.*

If we are going to follow Jesus' instruction to pray "like this," we need to count the cost. If we're not willing to offer angellike obedience to the Lord, we might as well get up off our knees. We're not praying the way Jesus taught us to pray. As James said, "You ask and do not receive, because you ask amiss, that you may spend it on your pleasures" (4:3). God's response to our prayers must compliment His program. Prayer is not to get God to conform to us but to seek His face in getting us to conform to Him.

Now the Lord's Prayer moves from worship into petition—for our physical needs, our spiritual needs, and our emotional needs.

Principle Four: Ask and If It Is Good You Will Receive It

"Give us this day, our daily bread." Notice that Jesus did not say, "Give us this day a Mercedes Benz." He was teaching us to pray for sustenance, not opulence. If all God hears from you is, "Give me this money," "Give me this home," "Give me this job, power, social status," you have missed the point of prayer.

Does this mean that we are not supposed to bring our desires before our heavenly Father? Of course, not!

There is a great statement about which prayers the Father will and will not answer in Matthew 7: 7–11: "Ask, and it will be given to you; seek, and you will find; knock, and it will be opened to you. For everyone who asks receives, and he who seeks finds, and to him who knocks it will be opened. Or what man is there among you who, if his son asks for bread, will give him a stone? Or if he asks for a fish, will give him a serpent? If you then, being evil, know how to give good gifts to your children, how much more will your Father who is in heaven give good gifts to those who ask Him!"

Those are very, very powerful verses of Scripture because they simply say, "Ask." Asking is not a difficult thing to do. In fact, if you have children, you know that they are almost constantly asking. When was the last time your child came to you and said, "Dad, Mom, what can I do for *you* today?"

Well, God invites His children to be children. Ask, seek, knock. And if those statements are not staggering enough, notice to whom He delivers that invitation: everyone!

The natural reaction at this point is, "Wait a minute! I've been asking for years. I've been knocking longer than that. And I've been seeking, and I haven't found anything. Anyway you just said that Jesus was teaching us to pray about sustenance, not opulence."

Isn't this a contradiction? Doesn't this passage offer an open-ended promise of provision? Not quite. That's why reading the Bible in context is so important. Look again at verse 9 and pay special attention to the two comparisons: bread and fish to stone and snake. What is the point? Very simply, bread and fish are good for you; stones and snakes are not. The earthly son has requested two good items, the earthly father responds accordingly. The reverse is also true. If an earthly son asked for a stone to eat, any loving father would refuse. (Everyone needs minerals in their diet, but this goes a bit too far!)

To follow through with our analogy, God is *not* saying, "Ask for whatever you want." Instead, He is saying, "Ask for what is good." When you ask for good things, our heavenly Father will surely approve—and He will never substitute something harmful. If you have prayed for something you desire with all your heart and have not received it, it is because this desire is either not good or not good *for now*. God is either saying, "No" or "Wait."

You may say, "But wait a minute. My circumstances *right now* are miserable. Everything I touch is falling apart; my world is crumbling. I've been praying faith-fully about it, and I've heard nothing! If God does not give His children stones or snakes, why doesn't He act on my behalf?"

Let me suggest that you read Romans 8:28: "And we know that all things work together for good to those who love God, to those who are called according to His purpose."

If you love God from your gut, then I have some good news for you. The mess you're in today will become your trophy tomorrow.

I have watched my wife cook about fifteen different dishes for the holidays, including several desserts. (And I have tried all fifteen of them at one dinner!) When she is mixing the cake batter, it's messy, gooey—anything but appetizing. Then, she pours the batter into the pan. It starts to take shape, but it is still little more than a partially coagulated mess. Finally, she puts it into the oven. Given enough time in that crucible of pain and anguish and burning, a delicious cake will emerge.

If you love God, it doesn't matter how hot the oven may be. When the allotted time is over, the same people who paid little attention to you while you were dough will wonder where this delicious looking pastry came from.

Ask. Ask! Ask and you shall receive!! But make sure that, to the best of your knowledge, what you're asking for is good. If it is, you shall receive. That's a promise!

How can you determine that your request qualifies for the "good" category? I suggest asking yourself two questions. First, is there anything in Scripture that justifies the request? For example, King Solomon asked for wisdom, and God granted him wisdom. The apostle James suggested that first-century Christians do the same. He said, "If any of you lacks wisdom, he should ask God, who gives generously to all without finding fault, and it will be given to him" (James 1:5).

Now suppose that there is no direct biblical support for your request. (It's a desire instead of a need.) While there's nothing necessarily wrong with this, it does bring us to our next question: "If God grants my request, what will He get out of it?" How will He be glorified and in what way will His Kingdom be promoted if He does as you ask?

You may be familiar with LeTourneau College, which is named after R.G. LeTourneau. He asked God to make him so prosperous he could live on 10 percent of his income and contribute the rest to the Lord's work (a sort of "reverse tithe!"). God not only answered his prayer, but provided so abundantly, the remaining 10 percent made LeTourneau a millionaire. But LeTourneau's request was rooted in his desire to glorify God.

King Solomon's request was similar. He asked God for wisdom instead of riches, because he knew he couldn't lead God's people without it. God not only gave Solomon what he requested, but unprecedented wealth as well.

Psalm 37:4 says, "Delight yourself in the LORD, and He will *give you the desires of your heart.*" Do you see the structure of this verse? It is built as an if/then statement: *If* you delight yourself in the Lord, *then* He will give you the desires of your heart. When we delight ourselves in the Lord, His agenda becomes our own. His priorities outrank ours.

A person who is delighted in the Lord may very well desire a house (or one of the other items I mentioned earlier). But he will pray, "Lord, give me this house so it can become *Your* house. Meet my need so I can build Your kingdom."

It is as though God is saying, "If you want My blessings so you can build a kingdom of your own, don't expect much. I'm only interested in answering the prayers of people who say, 'Thy kingdom come' and mean business."

Ask. If it is good, you shall receive.

We have prayed for our physical needs. Now we move to our spiritual needs.

Principle Five: Our Relationship with God and Each Other Must Be in Order Before Our Prayers Can Be Answered.

Jesus' next words were, "Forgive us our debts as we forgive our debtors. . . . For if you forgive men their trespasses, your heavenly Father will also forgive you" (Matt. 6:12, 14).

An electronic calculator is a very intriguing instrument, not only because of what it does but also because of what it can change (or "undo"). If we make a mathematical error, we simply press the "clear" button and all the improper data is eliminated from the calculator. We get to start all over again without trying to sort out the previous error. Not only that, the mistake is lost forever.

Such is the nature of God's forgiveness. Because of Jesus Christ's sacrifice on Calvary, the record of our sin is removed so we are no longer under condemnation by our Holy God.

There are five key Greek words in the New Testament for sin. Only one is used in the Lord's Prayer—

opheilema—which has to do with a balance owed. That's why, Jesus said, "Forgive us our debts," here.

Every time you sin, you go into debt to God. You have taken on an obligation you cannot possibly meet. It's like charging $100,000 to a credit card with a $1,000 limit when you have only a $1 bank balance. Sooner or later, the collection agency is going to come looking for you.

Sin makes us overdrawn debtors to God—even if we're already Christians. As a result, our fellowship with God is broken. Only confession and forgiveness can balance the books.

But this is only half the story. There's a condition in Jesus' model of prayer. God forgives our debts "as we also forgive our debtors."

Just as we can sin against God, others can sin against us. How we deal with those debts will set the stage for how God handles our "balance due."

Jesus told a parable about a king who wanted to settle accounts with his servants (see Matt. 18). A man who owed him several million dollars was brought to him. Because he was unable to pay, the king ordered the man's wife, children, and all his possessions to be sold. As these instructions were being given, the man dropped to his knees and asked for an extension. "Be patient with me," he begged, "and I will pay back everything I owe."

Now, a gracious king might have granted the man's request and set up a payment schedule with interest compounded daily. Not this king. He was so moved with pity that he *forgave the entire debt!* "Forget it," the king said. "The money is yours."

Soon after that, we read, the servant saw a fellow servant who owed him a few measly bucks. Grabbing the man by the throat, he demanded payment. "Be patient with me and I will pay you back," came the reply. (Doesn't that sound familiar?) But the servant refused. He had the man thrown into debtor's prison.

As you might expect, word of this incident reached the king. He summoned the servant and said to him, "You wicked servant. I canceled all that debt of yours because you begged me to. Shouldn't you have had mercy on your fellow servant just as I had on you?" The king reinstated the multimillion dollar debt and had the servant thrown into prison, where he probably spent the rest of his life.

Jesus wrapped up this parable with these words: "So My heavenly Father also will do to you if each of you from his heart, does not forgive his brother his trespasss" (Matt. 18:35).

If you're holding a grudge or refusing forgiveness (no matter how serious the offense) you can confess your sins until you're blue in the face, but God will not cancel your debt to Him. (In the end, you might wind up paying a price far greater than the person who wronged you.)

Jesus says that both our vertical relationship to God and our horizontal relationship to our fellow human beings must be in order for our prayers to be effective. He told His disciples, "If you bring your gift to the altar, and there remember that your brother has something against you, leave your gift there before the altar, and go your way. First, be reconciled to your brother, and then come and offer your gift" (Matt. 5:23, 24).

First of all, we pray for our physical needs—one day at a time. Then we pray for our spiritual needs, regularly asking for forgiveness and granting it. Finally, we pray for our emotional needs.

Principle Six: Keep Me from Situations That Will Be Too Tempting.

Next, Jesus told us to pray, "Do not lead us into temptation, but deliver us from the evil one."

Those words might seem to contradict what we already know about God because James 1:13 tells us God will not tempt us. How can Jesus say, "Do not lead us into temptation" when the Bible says there is no sin in God? Are we saying that if we do not pray, God *will* try to trip us up somehow? Of course not.

Jesus was really telling us to say, "Lord, as I live out this day, keep me away from situations that might cause me to wind up sinning—even though there may be nothing wrong with the situations themselves."

This is a cry of the emotions, similar to Jesus' own prayer in the garden of Gethsemane: "If it is possible, let this cup pass from me" (Matt. 26:39).

You might pray, "Lord, I want to live this day for You. Here I am on my way to work, and the folks there will try to get me to compromise my faith. I can handle some of them. But don't let me get in over my head. I don't want to compromise your Kingdom.

"Watch out for me today, Lord, so that even if people blow up at me, I won't go near the one who will make me blow up in return. I don't want to make You look bad. Lord, lead me down the paths that enable me to glorify You and resist the evil one. When You do that, Lord, You've taken care of my physical needs, You've taken care of my spiritual needs, and You've taken care of my emotional needs. So *Thine* is the Kingdom! Not, 'Thine *should be* the Kingdom,' not, 'Thine *will be* the Kingdom,' but, 'Thine *is* the Kingdom!' Your rule is what I want, You are the God I serve, and Yours is the name I will praise forever and ever!"

The Lord's Prayer is intended to be a pattern that all prayer should follow:

1. Pray for your physical needs
2. Next, pray for your spiritual needs
3. Finally, pray for your emotional needs.

We've looked at how we should pray. Now, let's look at the actual experience of prayer.

PRAYER PRECEPTS

What is God looking for when we come into His presence? Here are a few key precepts that make a difference in prayer.

Prayer Must Be Persistent

"Pray at all times," Paul told the Thessalonians.

In 1 Thessalonians 5:17, Paul admonished us to *"pray without ceasing"*. Paul did not mean that you must live like a monk on a mountaintop, spending twenty-four hours each day on your knees. Instead, he was proposing that you live in a constant state of communication with God. You are always aware that the channel between you and your heavenly Father is open.

Why is this constant contact so vital? Because Satan never sleeps. He is constantly seeking opportunities to attack, and we must be ready, through prayer, to don our armor and do battle. If you are the kind of person who prays only in the morning or just before bed at night, you leave yourself open to attack the rest of the day.

In Matthew 26, Jesus took Peter, James, and John with Him to the Garden of Gethsemane to keep watch while He prayed. He came back later to find them asleep. "Could you not keep watch with me for one hour?" He asked Peter. The subtle implication in Jesus' statement is that a full hour of prayer is not considered a long time. Everyone should have at least that much staying power. Yet most of us fizzle out long before sixty minutes passes by.

The regularity of our prayers is proportionate to the depth of our relationship with the Lord. Short prayers suggest a shallow relationship.

This same principle works in marriage. When partners stop communicating, the relationship is in trouble. I have had many wives sit in my office and say, "He does not talk to me anymore." The husband will shrug his shoulders and reply, "I don't have anything to say."

You can be sure he had plenty to say during their courtship. Back then, if he found himself without a topic, he would make one up. Or he would spend time telling her how beautiful she was or how much he loved her. He could not let the conversation lag. After all, she probably would not have married him if he acted like the bore he was later to become!

Jesus said "Men ought always to pray and not lose heart" (Luke 18:1). The implication is clear: If we don't pray we will faint. Prayer is a lot like breathing for people who make it a natural way of life. For believers who are growing in their faith prayer is a constant state of the heart, forever ready to communicate with the Father about any and everything.

As your relationship with the Lord grows more vital and dynamic, your prayer life will flourish as well. To pray without ceasing will become a natural, effortless expression of who you are.

Prayer Requires That We Heed the Signs.

Since you have probably never seen me drive, take my word for it—it is a sight to behold! One of my driving habits is riding on fumes. When the gauge approaches the "E," I assume that means "Enough to get me where I am going." Running on empty requires a delicate combination of hope and luck—and it does not take much to upset that balance!

Many of us live our Christian lives on fumes. We know that our spiritual tank is empty, but we try to push on anyway. After all, how could God allow a nice person like me to run out of gas when Satan is gaining on me?

I received the answer to that question a few weeks ago when my car began sputtering and finally coasted to the side of the road.

I prayed, "Jesus, I am here on the highway and there is not an exit in sight."

But, of course, it was too late. No angel was going to show up and put a "tiger in my tank." Why? Because I failed to watch the signs. I could not turn to God and ask, "Why did You do this to me?" I did it to myself.

Many of us allow our marriages to run out of gas before we consider spiritual refueling. When the relationship is coasting off the highway toward divorce court, it is often too late to start thinking about spending time in prayer, reorganizing priorities, and restructuring the family to match God's blueprint.

The same principle applies to every other area of life. Once you disregard God's purposes and God's guidelines, you can count on winding up on the side of some highway, sooner or later. Be watchful; make prayer a dynamic part of your life.

Prayer Must Not Be Selfish

I am not saying that prayer for yourself is inappropriate since Paul says that prayer is a part of putting on the armor of God. We *must* pray for ourselves, but not *exclusively* for ourselves.

I suggest a hierarchy of prayer that goes something like this. First, pray for yourself (your physical, emotional, and spiritual health, as I mentioned earlier). Confess your sins, and make sure your heart is oriented toward the purposes of God. Next, pray for your family. These are the people whom you are most likely to influence, and for whom you are responsible. Then, move on to your Christian relationships: your church, your brothers and sisters in Christ, who are not part of your nuclear family, but are part of your spiritual family. Check out the church prayer list to find out who is sick or in need. If you hear about a believer who is struggling or suffering, pray. I have witnessed miraculous healing in which God supernaturally intervened.

WHAT CEILING?

If we follow Jesus' model in The Lord's Prayer, no ceiling can stand between us and the throne room of heaven. Don't let Satan trick you into giving up the priceless privilege of communicating with our Creator.

The bottom line is *pray*. If you're tired, sick, emotionally overwhelmed—pray. If you're on Cloud Nine and life seems perfect—pray! If you lack direction—pray. If you doubt that prayer makes any difference—pray. If the circumstances of your life are out of your control—pray. If the circumstances of your life seem well within your control—pray even harder. Whatever you do—pray.

8

THE COMPLETE ROSTER: THE IMPORTANCE OF THE LOCAL CHURCH

I CAN'T TELL you how often I've heard people say, "I don't have to belong to a church to be a Christian. I can worship God in my heart."

That's sometimes a difficult challenge to refute because it happens to be true—to a point.

Nothing you do—and nothing you can join—makes you a Christian. The Bible makes it abundantly clear that Jesus is the only Way; no one comes to the Father except through Him.

So what *is* the value of the church? Is participation a prerequisite for growth as a Christian? Is it a mandatory part of maturity?

To find the answers to these questions, we'll refer to the book of Hebrews—an epistle written to a group of Jewish believers, who, in the face of severe persecution, were on the verge of defecting from the faith. The author of Hebrews suggested an alternative: "Let us hold fast the confession of our hope without wavering, for He who promised is faithful. And let us consider one another in order to stir up love and good works, not forsaking the assembling of ourselves together, as is the mannger of some, but exhorting one another, and so much the more as you see the Day approaching" (Heb. 10:23–25).

The book of Hebrews is probably second only to Revelation on the list of the Most Difficult Biblical Books to Understand. Making complete sense of it requires a thorough comprehension of Old Testament customs and theology, most notably the concept of the *covenant*. A covenant is a divinely established, legally binding relationship between two or more parties who agree to function under a designated structure of authority in accordance with revealed guidelines, resulting in long-term consequences.

Obviously, there's enough meat in this definition to fill a book of its own. For the purpose of our discussion, however, let's focus specifically on how to establish this covenant relationship with God.

In Old Testament times, the sins of mankind were temporarily washed away by the blood of sacrificial animals offered in accordance with laws and customs laid out by God. But when Jesus gave His life on the cross, He became the "Mediator of the new covenant" (Heb. 9:15) in which our sins are cleansed not by the blood of bulls, goats, and sheep, but by the sacrifice of a Savior.

The church, then, is the "community of the covenant," the assembly of those who share in the sacrifice of the God's Son.

It is important to understand that the benefits of our relationship with Christ are only realized *within* the context of this covenant community, in the same way that children have a greater length and quality of life if they keep covenant with their parents through obedience (Eph. 6:1–3).

Paul made this clear to the Ephesian Christians. He told them they could only experience spiritual growth if they were linked with other believers (Eph. 4:12–16). On the other side of the coin, God promised to judge those who brought harm to the church (1 Cor. 3:16–18). A certain level of personal care and support can only be realized in the dynamic relationship of the local church (1 Cor. 12:18–20, 25) and God's powers over Satan can only be fully experienced in the context of the covenant of the church (Eph. 3:10).

Here's the point: *Our relationship to the corporate body of Christians is crucial to the progress of the growth of our personal relationship with God.*

Against this backdrop, let's examine Paul's admonition in Hebrews 10: 23–25. He said, first, "Let us hold fast the confession of our hope."

"Let Us Hold Fast the Confession of Our Hope"

"Don't back down," Paul told the persecuted Christians in Jerusalem. "Stand up for what you believe, rather than giving up."

Some of us are very public about our faith on Sunday morning because it requires no risk. We applaud, say "Amen!" or get visibly excited because we're in "safe territory." On Monday morning, however, Dr. Jekyll often turns into Mr. Hyde—a spiritual schizophrenic who fits in all too well with his worldly workplace or social setting.

Can you imagine how God feels about this kind of weekly about-face? Put yourself in His shoes. Picture yourself dating a person who holds your hand affectionately in private, then drops it like a hot potato whenever someone else is around. While some might excuse this behavior as shyness, you probably see it for what it is. "You're ashamed of me," you say—and rightly so.

Jesus wants His relationship with us to be so strong that we won't mind if people see us publicly holding His hand. As children of the King, we must not be ashamed of our royal heritage. Then Paul suggested the way to endure persecution: Let us not forsake the assembling of ourselves together.

Let Us Not Forsake the Assembling

Remember, Paul was addressing a group of believers who faced serious opposition. Traditional Jews harassed them for their Messianic beliefs. The community at large ridiculed their morality and laughed at their lifestyle. And all the while, they could see the "day drawing near."

I believe the day in question took place in 70 A.D., when the Roman General Titus invaded Jerusalem, destroyed the Temple, and slaughtered thousands of Jews.

The religious community, the "folks in the neighborhood," and the political establishment were all against them. No wonder so many Hebrew Christians considered defecting from the faith!

What was Paul's prescription for spiritual survival in the midst of such oppression? Approach the throne with confidence, live the Christian life with boldness, and, "not forsake the assembling together."

This brings us to a key point. Why do we need the church? *To keep us from defecting from the faith.*

Remember the half-truth I quoted earlier? "I don't have to belong to a church to be a Christian."

As I said, that is true.

But from the moment you profess faith, Satan goes to work, trying to lure you into turning your back on Jesus Christ. He won't be satisfied until he renders you ineffective.

No, you don't have to go to church to be saved. Yes, you can worship God in your heart. But you *do* need the church to keep you on track. You *do* need the church to hold you accountable. You *do* need the church to care for you during the disasters of your life. You *do* need the church to encourage you as you keep walking down the right way. *You don't need the church to be saved but you need it to make sure you're living like you're saved.*

Why? Because *none* of us is immune from falling—not you, not me. No amount of study, experience, or theological training can make us fail-safe. During the past few years many preachers have learned this lesson the hard way. The apostle Paul was keenly aware of this fact—and he was about as spiritual as any man in history. "I discipline my body and bring it into subjection," he said, "lest, when I have preached to others, I myself should become disqualified" (1 Cor. 9:27).

Finally, Paul told the Hebrew Christians, "Stir up love and good works."

"Stir Up Love and Good Works"

Have you ever tried to build a fire with a single log? Once the kindling burns out, the fire slowly dies, leaving behind a few smoldering embers and some smoke. However, just add a few extra logs and some fresh air, then watch the flames erupt!

The church works on the same principle. Week after week, people stumble into church depressed and defeated. Then the choir sings, the pastor preaches the Word, and everyone praises the Lord. Slowly, the outlook brightens. Why? More logs on the fire combine with the fresh air of the Spirit to burn brighter!

The church needs each of our sparks to keep the fire burning. Now, there's nothing wrong with expecting a blessing from the Lord when you worship Him, but we must not forget the needs of others within the family of faith.

Putting the Family in Its Place. The story is told of four people in the church whose names were Everybody, Somebody, Anybody, and Nobody.

The church needed help meeting its financial obligations and Everybody was asked to participate. Everybody was sure that Somebody would do it. Anybody could have done it. But you know who did it? Nobody. It ended up that Everybody blamed Somebody when Nobody did what Anybody could have done.

When the church grounds needed some work, Somebody was asked to help. But Somebody resented being called upon because Anybody could have done it just as well. After all, it was really Everybody's job. In the end the work was given to Nobody, and Nobody got it done.

The process went on and on. Whatever the task that needed to be done, Nobody could be counted on to do it. Nobody visited the sick. Nobody gave liberally. Nobody shared his faith. In short, Nobody was a very faithful member.

Finally, the day came when Somebody left the church and took Anybody and Everybody with him. Who was left? Nobody!

You see, as members of the body of Christ, we are like the pieces of a jigsaw puzzle. Each piece has protrusions and indentations. The protrusions represent our strengths (gifts, talents, abilities) and the indentations represent our weaknesses (faults, shortcomings, undeveloped areas). The beautiful thing is that when we assemble, each piece complements the other, blending inconspicuously to produce a beautiful picture.

A healthy body requires harmony, unity of purpose, and a unanimous commitment to getting the job done. How do we develop such a robust body of believers?

Let Us Consider Ways. Paul told us to develop a strategy to stimulate love and good works. "Come up with a plan," he admonished.

If we are to truly look out for one another, it will require a plan. Each of us has a limited supply of time, energy, and resources; therefore, it takes everybody's doing a little, not a few doing a lot. Heaping the burden of care on a few faithful souls is a surefire path to burnout.

Instead, let us strategize *now*—*before* our friends defect from the faith. Let us develop plans to go get them. I believe four objectives should be part of every Christian's game plan.

1. Be Sure to Intervene before It's Too Late. Some of our family members have gotten so lonely, they're in danger of defecting from the faith. Go get them!

Some face emotional, economic, or medical crises. Go get them!

Some are married to nonbelieving spouses and experience so much conflict, they straddle the hedge of defection. Go get them!!

Intervene with care and compassion, but *intervene*. Wouldn't you do at least as much if one of your children was going astray? Or would you simply say, "I sure hope he turns around someday"?

What about those involved in sin? Galatians 6:1 tells us that some believers get "overtaken in many trespasses." I'm not talking about the rebellious person who lifts up what the Old Testament calls a "high hand" against God. Some of us are simply caught in circumstances we cannot seem to change.

A young man struggles with a drug habit. He wants to break free, but the chemical has gained so much control. He's caught.

A young woman has wandered into a morally compromising situation. She doesn't really want to be there, but she isn't sure of the way out. She's caught.

Whatever the circumstances, we can easily become tangled up in our own emotions and attitudes and habits and fears and failures and . . . we're caught.

"You who are spiritual," Galatians 6:1 tells us, "restore such a one in a spirit of gentleness." In other words, go get them!

When we're caught, we need somebody to yank us free and treat our wounds. *That's the job of the church.*

Outright rebellion, of course, is a different story. "I don't care about God. I'm going to live my own life and do what I want to do. I'm tired of doing right." That's the sound of rebellion. Rebellion demands discipline. But if I get caught—*really* caught—untangle me. Don't kick me. Untangle me!

And if a church member is rebellious, the church should also be involved.

2. Be Sure to Come Alongside Undisciplined Christians.

The disciplined individual controls his passions instead of being controlled by them. But what about the new Christian? Or longtime believers who are just recognizing the importance of putting their passions in their place?

That's where the church comes in.

It is a generally accepted fact that babies don't raise themselves. They need care, supervision, and guidance in order to grow into mature adults.

Baby Christians are no different. They can't grow without help. Spiritual growth occurs within an environment of loving accountability—precisely the atmosphere that should exist within the local church.

Jesus personally trained the original disciples. Then, He turned that job over to His body, the church. Each of us functions as a cell in that body, dividing and reproducing over and over again as we participate in the growth process.

However, in order to stay healthy, the body requires more than the reproduction of cells. It needs antibodies to protect it from disease. A doctor once explained to me that inside all of us, viruses and renegade cells occasionally pop off and begin doing their own thing. Soon, they start affecting (or infecting) the cells around them. Before long a tumor, a cancer or some other disease, develops. The result would inevitably be fatal, if not for antibodies. Antibodies are specialized cells that hunt down these renegades and destroy them before they destroy you. You don't have to think about it; it happens automatically in a healthy body.

In a healthy church, the process is remarkably similar. When renegade church members bring the infection of discord, disunity, or immorality, the right cells automatically go to work to fight the disease.

Why is the church so critical? In 1 Timothy 3:14, 15, Paul put it this way: "These things I write to you, though I hope to come to you shortly; but if I am delayed, I write so that you may know how to conduct yourself in the house of God, which is the church of the living God, *the pillar and ground of the truth.*" It's fairly obvious that the world no longer holds truth in high regard. Out in the world, games are being played; there's a lot of shuckin' and jivin' going on. But there's not much truth.

The church should be the one place where you can count on finding the truth, the whole truth, and nothing but the truth, so help you God. The quest for God's truth should be at the top of the list of what draws you to church on Sunday mornings.

In addition, there's a relational side to this equation. Every part of your body is in dynamic relationship with all of its other parts. If you were to cut off your leg, how far could it walk? If you cut off your hand, how well could it write? Once a part of the body is severed, it can no longer perform its function. It ceases to grow and develop. My hand moves only because it is physically connected to the rest of my body and, by means of the nerves, to my brain. Everything is interconnected and functions as a unit.

The church is a body that functions in dynamic relationship. A church can't grow around one person because no one person has everything another person needs. That's why we see an emphasis on small groups in the New Testament. This context facilitates encouragement, supervision, mutual support, and accountability. Without it, we are just a loose-knit association of individuals, and the process of spiritual growth is short-circuited.

We must develop caring congregations capable of coming alongside the weaker believers and help them develop discipline.

3. Be Sure to Encourage Each Other. Paul told the Hebrew Christians, "Do not forget to entertain strangers, for by so doing some have unwittingly entertained angels" (Heb. 13:2).

When Paul mentioned strangers in this passage, he was not talking about people off the street, vagrants who could rob or kill you. The context suggests he was referring to strangers *within the body of Christ.*

Are some of these strangers angels? Translated from the Greek, the word *angel* means "messenger." God's solution to your problem or provision for your need may have been in your midst all along. Yet you may have been living like a spiritual hermit, avoiding the church and cut off from a potential source of enormous blessing. And what about the times God might want to use *you* as His messenger?

Don't give up meeting together. Instead, encourage one another. Build one another up.

Not too long ago, on a day when I was feeling a little blue, I got a little note from one of my deacons. Suddenly, my day turned around. The note wasn't especially eloquent. There was no check inside. It simply said, "The sermon you preached this Sunday hit the target. It helped me overcome a problem I've wrestled with for years."

Wow! God used me to help somebody else! All of a sudden, I felt better. The message of encouragement in my sermon triggered *his* message of encouragement to me. Both of us are better for the experience.

The world specializes in tearing us down, not building us up. Climbing the ladder of secular success requires climbing over people, learning how to stomp on their fingers when their grip is weakest. But that's not how it is supposed to be in the church. We're called to be professional encouragers.

I'm not suggesting that you lie. Don't tell folks they're living right when they're obviously living wrong. Instead, give them the encouragement they need to start living right.

Is someone starving for that encouraging word stuck in your throat? It doesn't take a lot to make someone else feel better. And that's what the family of God is supposed to do: make people feel a whole lot better, and help them go on a little further.

A friend and I were lifting weights one day. I selected a barbell just a little heavier than usual. When my arms were only half extended, I knew I was in trouble—I couldn't push it any higher. All my grunting and sweating didn't seem to help; I was stuck!

My friend saw my problem and came alongside me. "Come on, come on," he said. "You can do it."

I appreciated the sentiment, but I knew he was wrong.

"Just a little bit more," he said, cheering me on. He put his hands under the bar, as though he was going to help me lift. (Actually, he was probably getting ready to catch the weight when I dropped it!)

"I've got it," he reassured me, "but you can make it." Finally, my arms extended and the weight went up. I was ready to give up at the first sign of muscle strain, but my friend convinced me I could succeed.

There are couples in our churches who don't believe their marriage can make it. They need someone to come alongside them and show them an alternative to divorce.

There are some singles who think that maintaining their moral purity is impossible. They need some successful singles to take them by the hand and show them the way.

There are young people whose families have disintegrated. They'll turn to drugs, gangs, crime, or prostitution unless someone stands beside them and offers to lead the way.

This is the definition of a church: *a community of believers who'll convince you you can make it, then stand beside you while you try.*

Every family makes occasional mistakes; the church is no different. Hurting people are sometimes overlooked. Signals are misread, wires get crossed. Yet the measure of a church is the effort it puts into preventing defection from the faith by caring for people—not the expanse of its buildings, the acreage of its property, or the size of its congregation.

4. Hold Each Other Accountable. When I was playing football, I often came home very tired and irritable, especially when we were having two practices a day (one in the morning and another in the afternoon). When I came home, I didn't want my mother to ask me to do anything. So as soon as I entered the house, I would bellow out, "I'm so tired, I think I'll go upstairs and rest." Now what I was saying to my mother, who couldn't help but overhear me, was, "Please don't ask me to do anything; I'm tired and frustrated and don't want to be bothered."

Do you think my mother cared? Absolutely not! She would respond, "Boy, you'd better get your big self in here and wash these dishes and clean this kitchen floor."

Still I'd retort, "Aw, Mom, I'm too tired to do all this stuff."

My mother would then respond, "Boy, if tiredness was a criteria of function, your breakfast wouldn't be cooked, your clothes wouldn't be washed or ironed, and your lunch wouldn't be made." But she didn't stop there. She went on to say, "Boy, if tiredness was a criteria of function, I would have gotten rid of you the day after your were born." (My momma doesn't mince words.)

Now what she was really saying was, "You are part of a family. You can't just enjoy the benefits of this home without also incurring equal responsibility."

Unfortunately, far too many Christians expect the opposite in their spiritual home called the church. Their attitude is "Preach to me, sing to me, pray for me, minister to me, but expect nothing from me." What's even worse, churches let members get away with this attitude of spiritual laziness.

In the same way my mother held me accountable for my responsibility to my family, church members must be held accountable for the proper use of their gifts and skills to build up Christ's body. This interrelationship among believers is called ministry. That may come as a surprise to people who still think that ministry is what preachers do. The Greek word, from which we translate *ministry*, literally means "service." *Every* believer is called to serve.

Imagine a collection of carpenter's tools holding a convention. Brother Hammer, who is presiding over the meeting, has been asked to leave because he is too noisy. Angrily, he replies, "If I leave, Mr. Screwdriver should come with me. He can't do his job without going around in circles."

Tall and slender, Mr. Screwdriver makes his way to the platform and counters, "I'm not the one who should leave. Look at brother Block Plane. His work has no depth; he never gets past the surface."

Now it's Brother Block Plane's turn. "What about old Sandpaper?" he replies. "He's so abrasive, he rubs everyone the wrong way!"

As the debate rages on, the Carpenter of Nazareth arrives to start His day's work. He puts on His apron and goes to His bench to build a pulpit from which to proclaim the gospel. He uses Mr. Hammer and Mr. Screwdriver, Mr. Block Plane and Mr. Sandpaper. In fact, He uses every tool in the shop.

Satan just loves to see us sniping at each other. The more he can make of our differences, the less aware we are of our true nature as God's tools designed by Him to accomplish a specific purpose.

UNWRAPPING OUR GIFTS

The apostle Peter told members of the early church, "As each one has received a special gift, minister it to one another, as good stewards of the manifold grace of God" (1 Peter 4:10).

Too many Christians either don't know or won't believe what Peter spells out clearly in this verse: *every* Christian has received, literally, a divine enablement, a gift. This gift may be a skill, a talent, a special sensitivity, or just an inclination. In any event, it is given with a purpose: to serve others in the body.

Pay special attention to the words *each one*. Those seven letters scuttle all excuses for ducking out on our duty to serve. Don't tell me you're unequipped, unqualified, or unavailable. Like every other believer, you have been divinely enabled and called to minister. To do any less is to reject God's grace and, in effect, to call Him a liar.

Let's consider a familiar Christmas Day phenomenon. Your children unwrap their gifts eagerly. Rather than buying duplicate presents for each child, you have purchased a variety of toys for your kids. Now you utter the word that makes the hair on the back of a child's neck stand up. "Share."

Sharing is about as popular among children as brussels sprouts. "Don't touch *my* stuff. Go play with *your own* stuff." That's when it's time for parents to play referee. You sit the children in neutral corners and explain, "Yes, it's your gift, but it is **your** gift in **our** house. After all, you don't live here alone. So, even though the package had your name on it, this gift was given to you with the understanding that it would be shared.

"Suppose the next time you asked me for something to eat, I said, 'No, I bought this food with my money. If you want to eat, go earn your own money and stop at the store on your way home.'"

Like the Christmas presents you give your children, God's gifts must be accepted and shared. They must implement God's plans and programs in your little part of the world.

Now, many people have unwrapped God's gifts and done something very interesting with them. For example, one person discovered that God had given her the ability to communicate with children in a way that helps them learn and understand. So off she went to visit the local school district. "I've got this gift of grace," she said, "and, if the price is right, I'll use it in one of your classrooms."

Another brother had a knack for numbers. So, with degree in hand, he marched downtown to a CPA firm and said, "Are you in the market for a gifted accountant? Well, I'll crunch numbers for you if you'll come up with the right number for me."

Is it wrong to use your gifts to make a living? Certainly not! Is it wrong to use your gifts to make a *comfortable* living? Not at all. Is it wrong to use your gifts to make a living, yet make them unavailable to God and His people for the building up of the Kingdom? You bet! If only the school district, the accounting firm, and the corporation are the beneficiaries of the grace God has bestowed on you, the Lord has been robbed.

MANAGING OUR GIFTS

Peter urges us to be good stewards of God's manifold grace, suggesting that we have the choice of being good stewards (managers over another person's property) or poor ones. In this case, the property in question is God's grace. Like your child's Christmas present, God's grace came in a package with your name on it, but it was given with the intent that it be passed on.

Acts 4:32 describes the characteristics of those who joined the early church in Jerusalem: "The multitude of those who believed were of one heart and one soul;

and *neither did anyone say that any of the things he possessed was his own,* but they had all things in common." What a perfect illustration of the concept of stewardship. The Christian has much, but owns nothing. I believe this applies whether we're talking about financial resources, personal property, or the special divine enablements God has given each of us.

Good stewards invest their abilities in the building of the Kingdom; bad stewards are in it for themselves, or aren't in it at all.

Good stewards watch God replenish their supply of grace so they are constantly empowered and enabled; bad stewards watch their allotment of grace stagnate like yesterday's manna and wonder why these other believers have all the enthusiasm and get all the breaks.

Think about it: If we're not dispensing grace, why should God provide more? Why bother keeping water pressure in the pipe if no one ever turns on the tap?

You may ask, "How do I get that water flowing?"

I answer, "Find a good church home."

FIND A CHURCH HOME

As long as churches are populated by fallible folks like you and me, there will be no such thing as a perfect church. But there are many good churches where you can learn and grow. If you don't currently belong to one, here are some tips on how to recognize them:

- A good church clearly proclaims the whole counsel of God as revealed in the Old and New Testaments of the Bible. A good church is a teaching church.

- A good church has a system of accountability within which people are held responsible for their lifestyle and disciplined when they unrepentingly rebel against God's standards.
- A good church has a comprehensive view of ministry. It applies the Scripture to every area of life and therefore has (or is seeking to develop) ministries that impact every member of the family.
- A good church provides opportunities for you to use your gifts and skills to serve others.
- A good church has a passion to win people to Christ and see them develop in the faith, and therefore it emphasizes evangelism and discipleship.
- A good church supports the weak, helps the needy, and encourages the downhearted. It prioritizes ministry to those who are less fortunate.

There is no place on earth like a good, Bible-centered church. Nowhere will you find better friends, quicker aid, or a more secure place of support and refuge during times of grief and tragedy.

Ask the Hebrew Christians. They took Paul's advice, and they learned, "I do have to belong to a church to continue to be a Christian in a world that's out to get me."

9

TEAM SPIRIT: THE GRACE OF GIVING

THERE'S A HUMOROUS story about a pastor who was preaching to his congregation about their need for progress. He started off by saying, "Children, if we are going to start moving forward as a church, we are going to walk."

A deacon sitting in the front row responded, "That's right, Reverend, let the church walk."

The preacher continued, "If we are going to move forward, next the church will have to run."

Again the deacon supported the pastor saying, "Yea, Reverend, let it run, let it run."

The preacher continued. "And after we run, then it's time to fly."

The deacon again affirmed, "Let it fly, Rev., let it fly." The pastor then said, "Well, it's time for the offering so the church can fly."

The deacon responded, "Let it walk, Reverend, let it walk." Unfortunately, this attitude permeates the church today. In fact, it is a travesty that the average giving of Christians in America is just two and one-half percent, much less than the minimum ten percent God expects from His people. Yet the objective measuring rod of our progress to spiritual victory is giving, "For where your treasure is, there your heart will be also" (Matt. 6:21).

THE NATURE OF STEWARDSHIP

One of the hardest concepts for people to realize is that we own absolutely nothing and God owns absolutely everything. God claims ownership of the whole earth and everything that lives on it (Ps. 24:1; 89:11) The Scripture says that everything good comes from God (James 1:17).

The reality that we are only stewards or managers, not owners, is mentioned by Solomon when he said, "As he came from his mother's womb, naked shall he return" (Eccl. 5:15). As the old adage says, "I've never seen a hearse pulling a U-Haul."

A good steward recognizes God's ownership and submits himself to it. A bad steward takes what belongs to God and uses it for his own selfish ends. The scope of stewardship includes our time, our talents, our resources, and our relationships—everything.

The privilege God has given us as stewards is akin to the president of a Fortune 500 company turning his firm over to an elementary school dropout. The dropout has done nothing to merit such a favor, yet the president has given him the company and makes himself available to show how to manage the business properly.

Having the mindset of a manager rather than that of an owner is no small thing. Spiritual victory or spiritual defeat hinges on which perspective you take, and that can be illustrated by looking at what happens when one buys his home rather than rents it. Most everyone wants to own his own home so he can have the freedom and independence he desires, answering only to himself for how he functions in his abode.

However, there are some advantages to renting rather than buying. When you rent and major things go wrong with your home—like the roof leaking, the water heater going out, or a pipe bursting—the landlord is responsible to fix them (assuming you have a good landlord). On the other hand, if you own your home and those same things occur, they become your problem because you are the landlord.

This is precisely how our lives work before God. If we seek to run our lives independently of Him, we are responsible to fix them when they break down. On the other hand, if we simply function as managers and recognize God as the owner of our lives, we can turn the broken parts of our lives over to Him and He will fix them. The truth of the matter is that life is too complex and Satan is too powerful for us to successfully run our own lives.

Stewardship of Our Financial Resources

Perhaps no stewardship issue has been so misunderstood among Christians as the subject of giving. The attitude of many churchgoers is clear (so clear some pastors steer a course around this subject to avoid the inevitable backlash): "You can say whatever you want about the state of my soul, but the moment you start messing with my wallet, I'm outta here!"

These brothers and sisters suffer from a disease called "cirrhosis of the giver," a malady discovered in

34 A.D. by a husband and wife team, named Ananias and Sapphira. This acute condition renders the patient's hand immobile when it is called upon to move toward wallet or purse en route to an offering plate. The strange symptoms are never seen in such surroundings as the golf club, the supermarket, the clothing store, or the exclusive restaurant. Some have attempted to treat this condition by pointing out certain tax deductions, which are available to patients in remission. However, the results of this therapy have been generally temporary and unreliable.

You might conclude that those afflicted with this disorder have a faulty understanding of the biblical doctrine of stewardship—the concept that God is the true owner of everything we possess and we are but managers of His resources. That assessment would be correct, but incomplete. A nongiving Christian misunderstands not only stewardship, but *grace*, because whenever you talk about finances, economics, or use of resources, you've traveled into the territory of grace.

You've no doubt heard it said that "it is more blessed to give than to receive" (Acts 20:35). Most of the people who quote that familiar phrase accept that it is probably more blessed to give, but they feel, deep down inside, that it is far more fun to receive. Their logic is based on the worldly assumption that giving involves losing and receiving involves getting.

To understand the flaw in that logic, you must be instructed in the economics of grace, which we talked about in chapter two. In an earthly bank, the amount of each check you write is deducted from your account balance. But not in that heavenly bank—the Bank of Grace. Each time you make a disbursement in the form of an act of love, a gift to someone in need, or a service to the church, the amount of that "check" is *credited* to your account. Service you withhold from someone else is, however, withdrawn. It is more blessed to give than to receive because giving increases the balance of your grace account. Keep giving, and the account will never run dry.

Unfortunately, most Christians only want to receive. They fall into one of three categories. The first is the "flint," which must be hammered on again and again, and even then all you get is some sparks and a few chips. The second is the "sponge." If you squeeze them hard enough, something is bound to drip out. The third is "the honeycomb," which just overflows with innate sweetness, releasing what it has stored up inside. Believers in this last category have understood the economics of grace.

That thought leads us to two particularly powerful chapters of the Bible: 2 Corinthians 8 and 9. You may wonder whether the subject of this part of Paul's letter is giving or grace. That's what makes this section so powerful. Paul saw the two as intertwined.

The Corinthian church had reneged on a financial commitment to send money to Christians in Jerusalem. Whether their gift fell victim to an economic crisis of some kind or simply got shelved in favor of another project, we do not know. Whatever the reason, Corinth had fallen a full year behind on its promise. In response, Paul not only reminded them of their commitment, but taught them a very valuable lesson about grace.

THE MOTIVATION FOR GIVING

The apostle Paul said something like this: "If you want to understand grace, check out your sister churches in Macedonia. Now, they're over on the other side of the tracks in the poor part of town. As if their deep poverty weren't enough, they are also suffering persecution, perhaps being abused because of their faith" (see 2 Cor. 8:1, 2).

Despite their circumstances, Paul went on to say that the Macedonian Christians overflowed with a wealth of liberality. Now, that seems like a contradiction. How in the world can the poor overflow with wealth? The answer is grace. Despite their economic condition, God had dispensed so much of His peace, His power, and His presence to them, they couldn't help but respond.

Paul was amazed by their commitment. He said, "For I bear witness that according to their ability, yes, and beyond their ability, they were freely willing, imploring us with much urgency that we would receive the gift and the fellowship of the ministering to the saints" (vv. 3, 4).

No professional fundraisers were necessary. No begging, no lotteries, no bake sales, no gimmicks. These folks wanted to give so desperately, they begged Paul for the privilege.

When was the last time you saw someone in your church stand up and say, "Don't go any further; I can't stand it. I've gotta give *now*. Somebody bring me an offering plate!" Can't you just see your pastor's jaw hitting the floor in amazement at the sight of just one believer so tickled to death with the idea of giving?

When we understand grace, our circumstances have nothing to do with giving. When we understand grace, our urge to give is not influenced by debt-to-income ratios, indexes of leading economic indicators, tax brackets, seasonal considerations, upward mobility, job security, or anything else. Instead, our giving is governed by our own need for grace.

When times are tough, we need more God, not less. We need more help, more Spirit, more peace, more power. The Macedonian Christians were caught in a crunch. The roof was about to fall in. They said, in effect, "Paul, we need some grace. Please accept this collection so God's grace can pour out and meet our deepest need. We want to write a check against our account in heaven because, more than ever, we need to build up our balance of grace."

The evidence of this accumulating grace is their abundance of joy, the one possession of which the Macedonians had plenty. You can do without quite a bit if you have joy. Without it, even riches can make you miserable.

It is not my intent to glorify poverty. I'm simply saying that God, in the abundance of His grace, enables us to cope with even the worst of circumstances by empowering us to live above those circumstances.

While I was going through seminary, my wife and I often wondered how we would feed our children the next day. Even hot dogs and beans were a delicacy we could scarcely afford on the meager $350 income each month. Only one financial plan seemed fail-safe: Set aside the Lord's money and give it first. Give it before making the house payment. Give it before thinking about paying school fees. Give it before buying hot dogs or beans. If we were going to survive, we needed to depend on God's resources. And in order to depend on God's resources, I had to make sure I was depending on God by faith.

We gave out of our need for grace. And God supplied faithfully, consistently, and often miraculously. There was money when we needed it, and there was joy in abundance. That joy gave me the strength to wait for His provision.

So don't tell me about a recession. Don't talk about lost jobs. Don't sing the familiar song of tough times and tight money. Christians write checks drawn on the Bank of Grace, not on the Dow Jones average. We depend on the provision of God, not the policies of the American economic machine.

Withdrawing from the Bank of Grace

Paul took a monetary inventory of the Corinthian Christians assets and pronounced, "[You are rich.] For you know the grace of our Lord Jesus Christ, that though He was rich, yet for your sake He became poor, that you through His poverty might become rich" (v. 9).

Congratulations, each of us today is also rich.

I know what you're thinking: *Where are all these riches I supposedly have?* They're plainly visible if you understand the biblical definition of riches: "To have everything you need to accomplish the purpose for which God has called you."

You know from our study thus far that God has already given you everything you need to become the person He wants you to be. Now it's our turn to follow the example Jesus set for us. It cost Jesus everything He had and everything He was to pour His deity inside of human flesh. Then, when He died on the cross for our sins, He wrote the biggest check the Bank of Grace had ever seen. Spiritual economics went immediately to work. "Therefore God also has highly exalted Him and given Him the name which is above every name, that at the name of Jesus every knee should bow, of those who are in heaven, and on earth, and under the earth, and that every tongue should confess that Jesus Christ is Lord, to the glory of God the Father" (Phil. 2:9–11).

And Jesus' check is to be shared by Christians equally.

The Equality of Giving

Jesus' sacrifice resulted not only in His glorification, but our sanctification—perhaps the ultimate "win-win" arrangement. That, in itself, is a vital point. Christian giving is not a scheme designed to comfort the afflicted and afflict the comfortable. The intent is to meet everybody's need simultaneously.

Paul made this very clear to the Corinthians: "For I do not mean that others should be eased and you burdened; but by an equality, that now at this time your abundance may supply for their lack, that their abundance may also supply your lack—that there may be equality" (2 Cor. 8:13, 14).

The Corinthian church was in serious disarray. They were arguing and fighting and cheating and taking each other to court. The men were sleeping around, visiting prostitutes, getting drunk. People were being caught in all manners of ungodly lifestyles. They loved to come to church, but they split up into factions when they couldn't decide whether Paul or Apollos was the better preacher. They were fairly well-to-do, but they lacked joy, they lacked harmony, and they lacked peace. In short, as I've said before, they were carnal Christians.

Meanwhile, Jewish Christians were starving in Jerusalem. They were rich in joy and secure in their faith, but desperately hungry. So, God orchestrated a trade.

The hungry Jews were fed from the Corinthians' surplus funds, while the Corinthians received a share of the joy with which the Jews overflowed.

Paul mentions this trade in verse 15: "As it is written, 'He who gathered had nothing left over, and he who gathered little had no lack.'"

Paul's Old Testament reference brings up an illuminating analogy. In Exodus 16, the source of his quote, the children of Israel were wandering in the wilderness on the way to the promised land. They were ravenous by this time and the possibility of starvation seemed quite real to them. Just when their prospects seemed most dim, God miraculously provided food in the form of manna, a fluffy white substance that fell to the ground—spiritual cornflakes from above. Along with the manna came a simple rule: You could only gather enough to meet your needs for one day. The only exception occurred on Friday, when you were allowed to pick up two days' worth of manna, since no manna appeared on the Sabbath.

As you would expect, people tried to hoard manna. After all, what if God changed His mind? It couldn't hurt to have a little extra on hand. Invariably, hoarders woke up to an unpleasant surprise: The manna had rotted and begun to breed worms.

What does this have to do with the link between giving and grace? A great deal. God has provided for all your needs out of the abundance of His grace. If you try to hoard the resources He has put under your control, it won't be long until you notice a distinctively distasteful aroma. God doesn't want you living on yesterday's manna. That's why the Lord's prayer says, "Give us *this* day, our daily bread." God wants you to walk with Him one day at a time. He wants us to trust Him for tomorrow, next week, and next year.

Now, you may have enough bread in your freezer to last you for weeks, but you still may be living on yesterday's manna.

Some Christians with beautiful homes have rotting marriages because they try to hoard God's blessings. Others have money in the bank, but can't stand to get up for work in the morning. It's not job stress or fatigue—it's a problem with rot. Malachi 3:8 poses the question, "*Will a man rob God?*" Perhaps the answer is now obvious.

The issue here is not money but how we respond to God's grace. God wants us to remember each day where our blessings, our forgiveness, and our very life come from. Lamentations 3: 22, 23 says, "Through the LORD's mercies we are not consumed, because His compassions fail not. They are new every morning."

It's much easier to share what you have today when you're sure that God will provide for tomorrow. And when Friday comes, you'll be equally confident that He also has Saturday covered.

I'm not advocating laziness. Cults have grown up around shiftless people who sit in groups waiting for God to provide. Instead, work as hard as you can, become as strong as you can, perform as well as you can. Along the way never lose sight of the fact that everything that comes your way comes from God to be shared, not stored.

Giving the Firstfruits

If we are giving to realize victory in the needs of our lives, then we are going to have to stop giving God the leftovers. You could give God one million dollars a week, but if it is the leftover million, it would be unacceptable to God. He is not honored when we fail to depend on Him, and whenever we take care of our affairs before acknowledging Him, we are in effect saying, "Lord, let me take care of me, then I'll take care of You."

This is why Proverbs 3: 9, 10 says, "Honor the LORD with your possessions, and with the firstfruits of all your increase; so your barns will be filled with plenty and your vats will overflow with new wine."

The concept of firstfruits continues even in the New Testament. Paul told the Corinthian Christians, "On the first day of the week let each one of you lay something aside" (1 Cor. 16:2). The Christians are to begin each week by worshipping God, which includes honoring Him by giving. Firstfruits does not mean that ten percent belongs to God while ninety percent belongs to us. A hundred percent belongs to God. Honoring Him with the first ten is saying, "Lord, because You have provided the first tenth of my crop, I want to affirm my trust in You for the ninety percent yet to come." Giving to God first is a downpayment, demonstrating that you are trusting Him to meet your needs in every other category of your life.

The truth of God's abundant grace and provision was driven home to Lois and me during those seminary days. I owned a 1971 Grand Prix. As I said, I made $350 a month and had three children (not exactly what you would call a windfall existence), yet we gave fifty dollars to God first. Quite a high percentage, but we recognized we needed all the divine help we could get.

My car was desperately in need of a tune up and I was tempted to use our offering for that month to pay for it. But after much thought, I decided, "No, I'm going to honor God first, and then trust Him to get my car fixed."

Soon thereafter, I saw smoke coming from under my hood as I was driving down the street. *My car was on fire!* I jumped out, ran to a phone, and called the fire department. As I waited to get my car towed, I was very upset with God.

Well, they towed my car in, and I had to find some money so that the insurance would pay to fix my car (since I had a two-hundred-dollar deductible). When I went to the dealership to check on my car, I casually mentioned I had to figure out some way to get the money for the deductible.

The service manager asked, "What deductible?"

I showed him my insurance papers.

He responded, "Sir, you didn't read these papers very carefully." Then he showed me where it was written in small print, *In case of fire, no deductible.*

You would have thought we were in church the way I shouted and carried on in that car dealership. I not only got a tune up, I got a new alternator, distributor, and wiring. My car was almost brand new under the hood, where it counted, and all it cost me was putting God first. I've never forgotten that lesson. Truly God can do "exceedingly abundantly above all we can ask or think" when we put Him first.

ACCOUNTABILITY IN GIVING

Paul warned the Corinthians, "I don't want to brag on you unless you're serious." Good intentions are fine, provided they result in good actions. He told them, "I realize that I don't even need to mention this to you, about helping God's people. For I know how eager you are to do it, and I have boasted to the friends in Macedonia that you were ready to send an offering a year ago. In fact, it was this enthusiasm of yours that stirred up many of them to begin helping.

"But I am sending these men just to be sure you really are ready, as I told them you would be, with your money all collected. I don't want it to turn out that this time I was wrong in my boasting about you. I would be very much ashamed—and so would you—if some of these Macedonian people come with me, only to find that you still aren't ready after all I have told them!" (2 Corinthians 9:1–4, TLB).

Just to make sure that the Corinthians fulfilled their pledge, Paul sent a delegation to Corinth. He held them accountable.

Christians get very angry when the church tries to hold us accountable. MasterCard, your car dealer, and the telephone company do it all the time; we expect that. At the same time we expect the church to be beholden to us for our gift, rather than expect us to pay it.

Some affluent people develop an attitude problem. They get the idea that the church is privileged to have them attend. "Treat me right," they say, "because I might take my tithe and my talent to the church down the street." These folks have it backward. The church is not privileged to have them; they are privileged that the church lets them through the door. Like all of us, they are what they are by the grace of God.

Again, there's nothing wrong with success. If God has provided you with an education, some talent, and some opportunities, praise Him! But since we're all recipients of God's grace, let's help each other respond to that grace in proper measure.

Biblical churches who hold their members accountable for their giving are not concerned about the size of an individual's gift, but that the gift is an appropriate response to the measure of God's grace. If you contribute $1,000 to the church out of your $10,000 weekly income, don't expect any extra credit from God. Yes, that is a lot of money. Yes, the church can do quite a bit with your tithe. But that doesn't buy you a pew with your name on it or a seat on the deacon board. From a grace perspective, your gift means no more or less than the dime dropped into the plate by the boy on a dollar-a-week allowance. Both of you are responding appropriately to God's providential grace.

Accountability is not an excuse to strong-arm the saints. Goading givers into giving robs them of an enormous blessing and reduces grace to cheap fundraising. Granted, doing the right thing under duress is still better than doing nothing at all, but the benefits God promises to givers are reserved for those who are motivated by a firm grasp of grace, not some guilt-induced sense of reluctant obligation. The Lord rewards those who realize, "Lord, if I weren't alive, I couldn't give. If my health were impaired, I couldn't give. Without the education You allowed me to receive, I could not have landed the job You provided, and I couldn't give. Everything, Lord, comes from You."

When you withdraw from the Bank of Grace an unbelievable thing happens, however. You also receive an automatic credit.

WITHDRAWING FROM THE BANK OF GRACE RESULTS IN AN INCREASE

I've said, "God responds to our giving with His grace." Paul promised this to the Corinthians: "And God is able to make all grace abound toward you, that you, always having all sufficiency in all things, may have an abundance for every good work" (2 Cor. 9:8).

You've heard stories (including some from me) about people who put their last dollar in the offering plate and received a generous payback from God. But some people tithe faithfully, give sacrificially, and remain poor. Has God failed to keep His promise? Or has there been some kind of cosmic delay?

You can count on the fact that God never forgets the faithful. Every check drawn on the Bank of Grace results in an increase. Sometimes that increase is seen in benefits you can't buy with money, like contentment. How many people would trade every dollar they had for genuine peace of mind? Elvis Presley, Marilyn Monroe, Janis Joplin, and others might have traded their talent, fame, and treasure for life instead of death if they really believed they could have peace—the same peace we enjoy through the sufficiency of God's grace.

If you could package healthy relationships and put them on supermarket shelves, they'd sell in a second. Everyone longs for vibrant, loving relationships—the kind that God's abundant grace enables us to develop.

Most people would pay any price for a sense of purpose. After all, what's left to live for if life loses its meaning? Those who understand God's grace realize how our lives fit into God's plan to build His kingdom.

On top of all these blessings, the Bank of Grace pays interest. The more you invest, the greater the dividend you receive. Or, to illustrate the point differently, "He who sows sparingly will also reap sparingly; and he who sows bountifully will also reap bountifully" (2 Cor. 9).

It is impossible to reap a forty-acre harvest from a single handful of seeds. But if you plant in proportion to your hope of a harvest, your forty acres of stalks will each be bent over with three, four, five, or more ears of corn. To a farmer, that's a bumper crop. To a banker, it's interest. To a Christian, it's the manifold grace of God.

Because God deals with us in grace, it is up to Him as to what our interest payments look like and in what form they come. So then giving is not a matter of making deals wtih God (as in prosperity theology); rather it is obeying God and trusting Him to meet our needs according to His riches in Christ as He sees fit.

I'm often asked by people going to our church, "Should we give from our gross income or from the net, after taxes?" I answer, "Do you think God blesses you from His gross or net?"

And I tell them, "Forget about the excuses and gimmicks."

No More Gimmicks

The church doesn't need more fund-raising events. It doesn't need to fry more chicken dinners or bake more cookies. It certainly doesn't need any more gimmicks or guilt trips. Our churches need believers who have grown enough in the faith to understand that giving is more than a matter of money.

Rest assured, the work of God which has been unfolding since the dawn of time won't come to a grinding halt if you pass the offering plate along without dropping in a check.

The Lord doesn't need your money. You need His grace.

PART THREE

CONFLICT— OVERCOMING THE OPPOSING TEAM

10

INTERCEPTIONS AND TURNOVERS: THE PURPOSE OF TRIALS

ANYONE WHO SERIOUSLY follows professional basketball would have to readily admit that Michael Jordan has radically changed the game. Many hold that he is the greatest player ever. Suppose Michael went over to the coach complaining, "Coach, please go over to the other team and tell them to leave me alone. They keep bothering me. Every time I dribble down the floor, they try to take the ball from me; and every time I try to shoot, they put their hand in front of my face so that I can't see the basket. I could do so much better if they would just leave me alone."

If Michael were to make such a complaint, it would fall on deaf ears. The coach would probably respond by saying, "Michael, we don't pay you megamillions of dollars annually for the other team to leave you alone. In fact, if they did leave you alone, the game would lose its excitement and anticipation, fewer fans would come, and you would, therefore, be paid less.

"Mike, the only reason we pay you all this money is so you can dribble the ball around your back and between your legs and make the other team look silly when they try to steal the ball from you. We want them in your face so that you can go up, over, around, and under the backboard—jamming the ball down their throats."

Opposition is necessary for Michael Jordan. And it's necessary for each of us as we live the victorious Christian life. It's necessary so we—and Michael—can show what we're really made of. God saved us to demonstrate to Satan and his followers what spiritual "slamma jammas" look like, and that can't be realized without testing. Trials, then, are a necessary part of experiencing victory.

THE TESTING OF OUR FAITH

Anyone who has been to school knows what it means to be tested, but few understand that, spiritually speaking, the true purpose of a test is to make you look good.

If you have studied the material in your assignment and prepared properly, the result is a foregone conclusion: You receive a reward in the form of a good grade and advancement. If you're prepared, your trials provide you with an opportunity to "strut your stuff!"

When circumstances turn against you and the deck seems stacked in favor of the enemy, it is just as though God is saying, "Clear your desk and grab your pencil. Here comes a pop quiz." God wants to know the same thing that your math teacher wanted to know: Have you assimilated the information He gave you to study?

There's no getting around it—exams make people nervous. Trials cause pain. But there's nothing like the rush you feel when you know you've scored big. God's given us a process for scoring big, despite the trials of our lives. Let's look at that now.

THE PROCESS FOR HANDLING TRIALS

Trials, tribulations, afflictions, ordeals, burdens, problems—call them what you will—are inevitable. The question is not whether you will be able to avoid trials but how you will handle them when they occur.

The apostle James set a lofty goal for believers beset with adversity. He said, "Count it all joy when you fall into various trials, knowing that the testing of your faith produces patience" (James 1:2, 3).

1. Count It Joy?!

Now, doesn't that sound a little bizarre? After all, peace is one thing. But how in the world can you have joy if your world is falling apart? Answer: You can't— not as long as you confuse joy with happiness.

Happiness is an emotion triggered by circumstances. It describes that bubbly feeling you get inside when everything is going your way. If I were to hand you a million dollars right now, you would likely feel happy. (Nothing like a quick million to brighten your day, right?)

Yet the happiest person alive doesn't necessarily have joy. Joy is more than an emotion; it is a deep, abiding sense of well-being that can sustain you even if you *lose* a million dollars. Joy is stability on the inside regardless of circumstances on the outside.

The Declaration of Independence asserts our right to life, liberty, and the pursuit of happiness. Yet being free to pursue happiness is no guarantee we will find it. Finding it is no guarantee we will keep it. And keeping it is no guarantee we will appreciate it. Why? Because emotions are transient, unpredictable, and undependable. God wants to give us more than a "reasonable facsimile" of satisfaction. He wants to give us joy. And that can be found from *knowing*.

I remember when Lois was in labor with our first child. There was no joy in the pain she felt. The joy came from *knowing* what the pain was producing. Two cells had joined together and blossomed into a brand new person who was about to enter the world. Though it hurt no less, the pain became tolerable simply because of the *knowing*.

The answer to godly suffering is *knowing*. We set aside what we feel in favor of what we know will occur. The author of James told the early Christians, "The *testing* of your faith produces patience." And he went on to say, "But let patience have its perfect work, that you may be perfect and complete, lacking nothing" (James 1:3, 4).

The story is told of a young boy who discovered a cocoon in a backyard tree. He studied the cocoon carefully, seeking some sign of life. At last, several days later, the boy saw what he had been waiting for. Inside the filmy shell, a newly formed butterfly was struggling to get out. Filled with compassion for the tiny creature, the boy used his pocket knife to enlarge the hole. Exhausted, the butterfly tumbled out—and lay there, without even trying to fly. The boy didn't know that the struggle to escape was designed to strengthen the butterfly's muscle system and prepare it for flight. His act of "compassion" had inadvertently crippled the beautiful insect and ultimately doomed it.

The night before He was crucified, Jesus prayed to His Father, asking Him *not* to take us out of the world, but to keep us safe *in* the world. The goal, Jesus realized, was not to steer around difficulty, but to navigate safely through it.

2. Be Patient and Allow the Process to Happen.

Letting patience have its perfect effect means that we must not lay down our pencils halfway through the exam. Even if we have answered each question correctly, quitting at the halfway point limits our score to 50 percent—an F at most schools. Like the butterfly in the cocoon, getting from point A to point B is not the entire agenda. The *process* of getting there is equally important.

Unfortunately, too many of us want to skip from kindergarten to college once we've passed our first test. "OK, I've taken a test. That's it; school's out!" That makes as much sense as your ten-year-old telling you he wants to be a brain surgeon—now! "I'm not interested in college, Dad. And medical school sounds like a drag too. But deep in my heart, I know God wants me to be a doctor."

Right? Wrong. That boy is foolish. He wants the benefits of the educational process without the accompanying responsibility.

God understands that the process is as important as the result. That's why He sometimes elects *not* to deliver us from certain situations.

3. Keep the Proper Focus.

James told us to consider it joy, which means we must process the information through our minds. And as we do so our focus becomes all-important.

This was vividly driven home to me the day I took my then young son, Tony, Jr., who was sick with asthma, to the doctor. Every time the doctor came near him, he broke out in tears. The wise physician reached into his pocket and pulled out a lollipop. My son's countenance immediately changed. He took his focus off of me, the doctor, and his asthma, and put it on the new joy in his life—the lollipop. Then the doctor eased over and gave him a shot with a long needle. My son began crying. All of a sudden, however, he looked at his lollipop again and forgot his pain.

When we are going through the painful trials of lives, Jesus is like that lollipop. If we focus on Him, our countenance changes so we experience joy in the midst of tribulation (Rom. 5:3–5).

Remember the time Peter walked on the water? (See Matthew 14:22–33.) He was doing fine, the Bible tells us, until he noticed the strong winds. At that point, he became afraid and began to sink. His focus had shifted away from Jesus. "You of little faith," the Lord remarked as he pulled Peter to safety, "why did you doubt?"

Remember the story of Mary and Martha? (See Luke 10:38–42.) One day, when the Lord visited their home, Martha labored to serve a lavish meal to Jesus, while Mary sat at His feet and listened to what He said. After a while Martha became angry at Mary for not helping, and she became angry at Jesus for allowing Mary to get away with not helping. Martha was a fight waiting to happen. She asked Jesus, "Why don't you send Mary to the kitchen to help with the preparations?"

Jesus disarmed her with His reply: "Martha, you are worried and upset about many things, but only one thing is needed. Mary has chosen what is better, and it will not be taken away from her." Let me paraphrase Jesus' words: "Martha, find your chief joy in me—not in the meal you're preparing for me."

I can hear echoes of that advice ringing in many ears:

- "Find your chief joy in Me, Pastor, not in the church you are trying to build for Me."
- "Find your chief joy in Me, student, not in that dissertation you're writing."
- "Find your chief joy in Me, employee. We'll take care of pleasing your boss together."
- "Find your chief joy in Me, single person, because no one can fulfill you like I can."

To rejoice is a choice. How will you perceive the reality of your life? Is your focus on Jesus?

A friend of mine was particularly disturbed because she had lost a major customer. That night she lay awake for hours—tossing and turning—until she turned her focus on Jesus, particularly *her* love for Him. As she did so, the feelings of fear and anger turned into feelings of love; she loved Him so much, her love dissipated those fears so she could finally fall asleep.

"But I'm having trouble focusing on Jesus," you say. "I can't see why He'd allow me to suffer so unjustly. I'm a victim, not a perpetrator."

Why?! I don't have the answers to the "why" questions; no one else does either, unless God answers them in His Word. If He talks about it in His word, I can give you an answer. If He doesn't explain it in His Word, I can only guess.

That was Job's situation long before God's Word was recorded for men to read and study. Job could only guess why he was undergoing so many trials and tribulations. Finally, he asked God directly to explain why he was being treated so badly.

In essence he said, "Why are You doing this to me, God? I'm righteous; I've always honored You. I've faithfully obeyed You. But what's my reward? My children are dead, my reputation is shot, I can't work, my house is gone, I'm sick as a dog, and most of my friends and even my wife have turned their backs on me. The three friends I have left can't explain what's going on, so I'm asking You: Why do the righteous suffer? Will You please explain Yourself?"

When Job asked God those questions, we are told that a whirlwind suddenly swirled around him, and he heard God's voice in it. If Job was expecting a soothing, gentle response, he certainly was surprised when the Creator answered him from that whirlwind: "Who is this who darkens counsel by words without knowledge? Now prepare yourself like a man; I will ask you, and you shall answer Me" (Job 38:2, 3).

God then gave Job a rapid-fire questionnaire: "Where were you when I was laying the earth's foundation? Can *you* command the sun to rise? Have you walked on the bottom of the sea? Can you number the clouds in the sky, or guide a wild bear and her cubs or feed the lions?" Do you remember Job's reply?

The Bible says Job was silent. He stood before God weak, ignorant, and humbled, because he had not existed when God created the earth. He had no power to make the sun rise or to count the clouds in the sky. He had never seen the deepest seas much less walked in their depths, and for a mortal man to think of handfeeding the lions was ridiculous. Job got the point.

Do you see what God was telling Job—and you and me? By these questions God was reminding each of us that He is the all-powerful Creator, the giver and controller of life. As He explained these things to Job, He made His troubled, but righteous, servant recognize that even when he couldn't understand the why, he could know the *Who.*

God was saying, "If you know Me, Job, that's all you really need to know." As the closing verses of the book of Job show, Job learned the lesson, began living according to it, and was blessed by God. Unfortunately, today some of us have forgotten the lesson or chosen to ignore it and are suffering the consequences of a defeated life.

The second ingredient in personal peace is a sensible lifestyle, which Paul called "a forbearing spirit." He wrote, "Let your gentleness be known to all men. The Lord is at hand" (Phil. 4:5).

4. Keep Your Lifestyle Sensible.

Phillipians could be called "the epistle on trials" since Paul dictated this letter as he was languishing under Roman imprisonment, awaiting a fatal verdict on crimes he did not commit. Yet the term *forbearing spirit* suggests flexibility. Lighten up! Nothings generates stress like rigidity. As we encounter life's twists and turns, those who cannot bend will likely break.

Learn to be flexible at work, at home, at school—wherever you are. If somebody crosses you, don't retaliate—be flexible. If your plans don't work out the way you intended, don't panic—be flexible. If you're facing impossible deadlines and there's no relief in sight, don't give up—be flexible. After all, the Lord is near! When Christ returns, proper justice will be dispensed, all plans will be changed, and all deadlines will be set aside. If you die from a stress-induced heart attack, the same applies. So why not be flexible? Not irresponsible, just flexible.

Include time in your schedule for proper rest and some recreation. Make sure that the pressures of your to-do list don't crowd out the things that are truly important, like Bible study, fellowship, and prayer.

Pray with a Thankful Heart. Prayer and supplication, Paul told us, should take place within the context of *thanksgiving.* How ingenious! In the midst of praying about our anxieties, Paul suggests thanksgiving, which instantly refocuses our attention on the positive side of our circumstances. You might pray, "Lord, do something about that boss of mine." Thanksgiving adds a new dimension to your prayer: "I am thankful you gave me this job, Lord. Through this job, you provided the means to buy this home, drive this car, and wear these clothes." In the context of all God is doing, your "boss trouble" seems like a smaller issue than it did at first.

5. Ask for Wisdom.

In order to be able to make wise decisions through-out tough times—and to truly take the first four steps—James suggested that early Christians ask God for wisdom. "If any of you lacks wisdom, let him ask of God, who gives to all men liberally and without reproach, and it will be given to him" (James 1: 5).

Wisdom, quite simply, is the ability to apply divine knowledge to life's situations. A knowledgeable man has stored away a load of information; a wise man knows how to draw on that storehouse to form answers or solutions.

Do you lack wisdom? Ask God! Too often, God is the last person to whom we turn for answers. God sometimes takes His place in line after the pastor, the elder, the deacon, the neighbor, and Aunt Mary's second cousin once removed. We fill the calendars of $150-per-hour psychiatrists, inflate the sales of quick-fix self-help books, and tune in to the likes of Oprah and Phil in our quest for answers. All the while, God is waiting to hand out liberal supplies of wisdom to all who ask.

God hands out wisdom "without reproach." He doesn't mind our repeated requests for spiritual insight, provided we ask in faith. James said, "But let him ask in faith, with no doubting, for he who doubts is like a wave of the sea driven and tossed by the wind. For let not that man suppose that he will receive anything from the Lord; he is a double-minded man, unstable in all his ways" (James 1:6–8).

Trying to weasel out of a God-given growth opportunity is an expression of doubt. "I can't pass the test, Lord. Let's move on to something else." When we pray in faith, we believe that God can and *will* give us the wisdom we need to make the grade.

Don't believe me; try it! Resist the urge to ask for an escape from the trial—ask for wisdom instead. Then watch God keep His promise. You'll reach a new height of spiritual excitement as you discover that the Word works!

"But I can't believe my problem is a God-given growth opportunity," you say. "How do I know that this is one of God's tests?"

My answer? God may allow trials in your life so you can "strutt your stuff," but He never tempts you. Let's look at the difference.

FROM TRIALS TO TEMPTATION

While God brings trials into the life of the Christian to prove, purify, and promote the corrective discipline of His children, He never leads His children into sin. James made this clear when he wrote, "Let no one say when he is tempted, 'I am tempted by God'; for God cannot be tempted by evil, nor does He Himself tempt anyone. But each one is tempted when he is drawn away by his own desires and enticed. Then, when desire has conceived, it gives birth to sin; and sin, when it is full-grown brings forth death" (James 1:13–15). To understand the difference between the trials of God, which are designed to lead us to victory, and the temptations of Satan, which are designed to lead us to defeat, one only has to observe automobile commercials.

When automobile manufacturers wish to show you how sturdy their cars are, they run cars through obstacle courses in all kinds of weather. However, when the opposition wishes to show the limitations of their competitors' products, they will film their own tests, showing the weakness of the other cars, so people won't purchase them.

or make them stronger. When the devil tempts, however, his goal is to bring about our defeat and embarrassment.

Yet God gives us a guarantee in such a situation. He makes it unmistakably clear that He, God, will provide the necessary directives to lead us to victory when Satan tempts us. Listen to Paul's words to the church of Corinth: "No temptation has overtaken you except such as is common to man; but God is faithful, who will not allow you to be tempted beyond what you are able, but with the temptation will also make the way of escape, that you may be able to bear it" (1 Cor. 10:13).

Paul was warning the carnal Corinthians that they were in danger of being spiritually disqualified, like Israel was, never experiencing God's full blessings in their lives.

You see, it was God's intention to test Israel's commitment to Him by sending them into the wilderness in the first place. He gave them a test. As Deuteronomy 8:2 says, "And you shall remember that the Lord your God led you all the way these forty years in the wilderness, to humble you and test you, to know what was in your heart, whether you would keep His commandments or not." God's purpose was to determine their obedience.

However, just the opposite happened. The Israelites allowed the enemy to dupe them into yielding to their lust, causing them to rebel against God. Satan tempted them and they responded.

The Corinthians faced the same dilemma and so do we. God leads all His children into wilderness circumstances to train us, humble us, and determine our obedience. However, He never leads us into a trial He has not given us the ability to handle.

God made us. He knows when enough is enough. The trials you face will be within your power to endure. The Lord may not allow us to elude a test, but He's not in the business of giving college entrance exams to first graders.

God limited what Satan could bring into Job's life, in light of His knowledge of how much Job could handle, and God controls the amount that comes to us in the same way. He will not put more on us than we can bear or allow Satan or other people to do so either.

But we must remember: The escape God provides enables us to bear our trials, not avoid them. You may reply, "But what kind of an escape is it if we still have to bear those tough times?"

Paul's point was that God leads us successfully through difficulty, not around it. Just as Israel had to go through the wilderness, Christians must go through God's testing and Satan's temptations. This process allows us to verify our own commitment while we identify our weaknesses so we can overcome them and turn them into strengths.

A Brief Disclaimer

Let me add a disclaimer here. God said He will not allow you to be tempted beyond your ability to endure. That promise doesn't cover trials you bring on yourself—or those times when you give in to Satan's temptations. Some Christians seem bent on asking for trouble. If you rebel against the Divine standard and your life takes a turn for the worse, don't complain to God about the "trial" He has sent you. Trials you cultivate through rebellious behavior will not result in joy. They yield a very different—and disastrous—harvest. We'll talk about that in the next chapter.

The apostle Peter clearly distinguished between trials we encounter and those we manufacture. He said, "If you are reproached for the name of Christ, blessed are you, for the Spirit of glory and of God rests upon you." However, he went on to say, "But let none of you suffer as a murderer, a thief, an evildoer, or as a busybody in other people's matters" (1 Peter 4: 14, 15).

SPIRITUAL REPORT CARDS

In any test, there comes a time when the teacher says, "Put your pencil down and hand in your paper." Before long, the test will come back marked with a grade. In the spiritual arena, God grades our tests as well. At the end of this chapter James told us: "Blessed is the man who endures temptation; for when he has been approved, he will receive the crown of life which the Lord has promised to those who love Him" (James 1:12).

God reviews your performance in the midst of tough times and writes "Approved" next to your name. Many people believe the "crown of life" to be a victory wreath that God presents upon our arrival in heaven. But I don't believe God withholds His approval that long.

Remember when Abraham was instructed to sacrifice his son? He trusted God—even in the midst of potentially tragic circumstances. Just as he was about to plunge the knife into the chest of his child, the angel of the Lord stopped him. "Approved!" God said.

When your test is finished and you have passed, God rewards your efforts with the crown of life. What is life? John 17:3 tells us: "This is eternal life, that they may know You, the only true God, and Jesus Christ whom You have sent." Life is knowing God *now*, not just when we go to live with Him in heaven. Life is when God looks at your situation today, breaks through your wall of trials, invades your experience, and single-handedly turns your circumstances around. That's life.

You've been single for years, praying for a mate. Out of frustration, you've given up on dating and are resigned to living the rest of your years alone. Suddenly, out of nowhere, there he is—the man of your dreams (or, more precisely, your prayers). That's life.

You're unequally yoked to a nonbeliever. You've prayed for years that he would become the man God wants him to be. But God would not release you from the test until you learned to be the woman He wanted *you* to be. Faithfully, you applied the principles of submission and love. In time, God says, "Approved." Then, suddenly, your stubborn man confesses his sin and seeks a Savior. That's life.

Few experiences on earth match the excitement of seeing God turn trials into triumph. But that transformation is a *process*, not an *event*.

It takes the fire of the furnace to produce hardened steel. Only the intense pressure of the earth can create the precious diamond. And only our trials can produce the kind of Christian character God wants to build within us.

God establishes the curriculum in this classroom of life. There's no longer any need to cut class when testing time comes. Face the tests with confidence and consider it joy! Start living above your circumstances and experience the peace that passes all understanding. A cloud of witnesses will tell you you will be victorious.

The Cloud of Witnesses

Often, before a major professional fight, all the past champs are paraded through the ring. While the crowd applauds wildly, each one shakes the hands of the evening's contenders.

As the likes of Sugar Ray Leonard, Smokin' Joe Frazier, and Muhammad Ali offer their best wishes to the guys sitting in the corners, ready to fight that night, they are silently delivering an important message: "This is not the first championship fight in history. I sat in this ring once myself. Take it from me—you may leave here with a bloody nose, a bruised rib, or a broken jaw. But you may also leave with a belt. I'm living proof that this contest *can* be won."

Like the Hebrews, some of us have been beaten and bruised—if not literally, at least figuratively. Some have spoken out for Christ only to have our jaws broken. We've been bloodied in our battle with the world. It's only natural to ask, "Can this war be won?"

The answer, of course, is a resounding *yes!* provided we fight the fight, run the race, and live life by *faith*. To back up this claim, the writer of Hebrews offers proof.

Have you heard your preacher pause in the middle of a sermon and ask, "Can I get a witness?" He wants to know that his congregation is backing him in prayer and that they understand his point. When you want to find out who is backing *you* in your day-to-day struggles, you may want a witness as well.

Hebrews 11 tells us that we have *more* than a witness; we have a *cloud* of witnesses! (There's a regular storm brewing out there!)

"God," you may ask, "Who are these witnesses You are talking about?" The answer depends on your need.

Perhaps your problem is a health problem. "I'm sick," you say, "and my doctors haven't got a clue what's wrong." Well, there's old Enoch in the crowd, saying, "I'm your witness!" Enoch walked so closely with God, he never tasted death. Hebrews 11:5 (KJV) tells us he was "translated." Ask Enoch—he'll tell you that deterioration and disease have no dominion when God is in charge. "All right, but how long must I wait for God to come through for me?" Why look— isn't that Noah stepping up to the podium? "I'm a witness!" he shouts. "God told me it was going to rain. He didn't tell me it was going to take 120 years. I just knew He called me to be faithful." Everyone outside Noah's immediate family thought him insane. Even though people didn't listen, the giraffes did. And so did the camels and the goats and the lions and the butterflies. Noah and his family survived, and wound up inheriting the entire world.

You say, "But you don't understand, Preacher. My situation is impossible." Let me respond by introducing you to Abraham and Sarah. He was pushing 100, and she was just a decade behind him. God told them it was time to start a family. Today, we call that family the nation of Israel. Don't talk to me about "impossible." I've got a witness from Abraham and Sarah.

Let's hear a word from Rahab—the only person in Jericho to embrace the God of Israel. When the walls of Jericho tumbled down and the city lay in ruins, just one house remained standing, and it wasn't the local Holiday Inn. Yet Rahab's greatest testimony is found in Matthew 1, where she shows up in the genealogy of Jesus. God took this woman and made her *somebody*.

Witnesses like the ones I've mentioned can be a great encouragement. All of these people were special, but they were still just people. Abraham was immoral. Moses disobeyed God when he killed the Egyptian and, later, when he struck the stone with his staff. Rahab was a harlot. Each had a mark on his or her resume.

It is dangerous to become so intent on the illustrations that we miss the point they are intended to illustrate.

That's why Hebrews 12:2 reminds us to "fix our eyes upon Jesus" (NIV). I've mentioned this before in this chapter, but I'd like to remind you of it now. If you only remember one part of the process of overcoming interceptions and turnovers, let it be: Fix your eyes on Jesus.

Fix Your Eyes on Jesus

In driver training classes, instructors remind their students to "aim high." This is good advice. If you're staring at the road, trying to stay between the white lines just in front of your car, it's much harder to steer than if you look further ahead toward where you want to go. In life, we try too hard to steer between our circumstances. "Aim high," Jesus says. Keep your eyes on Him as you steer your way through life. That leaves no doubt about your destination, and tends to smooth out the road along the way.

Let's not forget that Jesus, "for the joy set before Him endured the cross" (Heb. 12:12). Jesus knew about the cross, but He did not fixate on it. He didn't want to go, but He refused to let that fact paralyze Him. He had his sights set on Sunday morning!

It is as though He said, "On Friday, My head will be dripping with blood from the thorns they will drill into My skull. On Friday, I'm going to have a hole in My side and My bones are going to jump out of joint. On Friday, all of humanity will mock Me and scorn Me. On Friday, My Father will turn His back on Me as I take the sin of the world on My shoulders. So I'd better not look at Friday. Let Me take a long, hard look at the joy of Sunday morning instead."

Brothers and sisters, get your eyes off Friday. I know you're bearing a cross. But I also know you have a risen Savior sitting at the right hand of the Father. Keep your eyes on Jesus.

Are you still not sure that will work? All right. Let's see if I can get a witness.

If the apostle Peter were here, he would tell you about that day he walked on water. As long as he stared straight at Jesus, putting one foot in front of the other, he did just fine. But then he got distracted by the storm and the waves. It could have been made worse by the shouts of the men back in the boat. Maybe he remembered something from a physics class that had to do with the density of water. Whatever it was, it was enough to change the story. He began to sink. Just as he was about to go under, he remembered to fix his eyes on Jesus.

"Lord, save me!" he cried. Because Peter redirected his gaze, he lived to tell the story.

Stephen, will you testify about whether fixing your eyes on Jesus can sustain you?

If Stephen were here, he would tell you that even though the Sanhedrin condemned him, he kept his eyes on Jesus. As the stones were fracturing his skull, he saw heaven open. As he looked at Jesus, he saw something more powerful than a rock!

How about the ten lepers? They could tell you how their flesh was disintegrating until they looked to Jesus.

But you don't have to look to the past for a testimony to the power of God. Ask your Christian friends, ask your pastor. Ask me!

I can remember when there was no food on my table. I can recall wondering how I could continue in the ministry. There were times when we didn't have the money to pay staff salaries at the Urban Alternative. In every case, we looked to Jesus. And, in every case, we found the strength and resources to carry on. I can testify that fixing our eyes on Jesus has brought us through every single time. He helped us make it, and He will help you make it too.

11

A BLITZ BY THE OPPOSITION: WAGING SPIRITUAL WARFARE

IN THE SUMMER of 1990, Saddam Hussein and his Iraqi army invaded the tiny Middle East nation of Kuwait. Hussein brought with him death, disease, and destruction, as he sought to expand his kingdom and authority throughout the region. Saudia Arabia, fearing it would be next on Hussein's "hit list," called the White House for help.

In one of the strong moves of George Bush's presidency, he mobilized over 500,000 men and women from countries all over the world to form one united front against Hussein and his army. This united coalition drew a symbolic "line in the sand" to serve notice on the enemy: "You have to withdraw your illegitimate claim in Kuwait and vacate the premises!"

In a similar way, Satan has invaded territory he did not create and does not own, bringing with him death, disease, and destruction. God has formed a coalition of His people, made up of all races, classes, and cultures, who have one overriding purpose: to serve notice on the enemy that he must vacate the premises.

The whole of the universe is divided into two rival kingdoms—the kingdom of light or righteousness, ruled by God, and the kingdom of darkness or evil, commanded by Satan. He is our enemy and our world is the battleground where his efforts to compete with God are played out. The apostle Paul warned the early Christians about this: "For we do not wrestle against flesh and blood, but against the principalities, against the powers, against the rulers of the darkness of this age, against the spiritual hosts of wickedness in the heavenly places" (Eph. 6:12).

Let's take a closer look at this spiritual battle and our enemies—the devil, the world, and the flesh—to see how they work to defeat us.

THE DEVIL

Satan is one of the most misunderstood beings in the universe. For some he's like a Disney character—entertaining and interesting, but not real. For others he's a diabolical force, with horns, a pitch fork, and a red jumpsuit.

The biblical picture of the devil is different. He is an awesomely powerful, brilliant, and crafty person, who spares no effort in subverting the plan and program of God in favor of his own. So powerful is the devil that other powerful angels, like Michael, would not even go against him (Jude 9).

As the highest of all of God's created beings, Satan's responsibility was to lead the angelic host in the worship of God. According to Isaiah 14:12, his name was

Lucifer, which meant son of the morning; and according to Ezekiel 28:12, he was perfect in wisdom and beauty. However, rather than being grateful to God for the opportunity and honor bestowed on him, he became arrogant and proud. The prophet Isaiah described Satan's attitude when he got the "big head":

> "For you have said in your heart:
> 'I will ascend to heaven,
> I will exalt my throne above the stars of God;
> I will also sit on the mount of the congregation
> On the farthest sides of the north;
> I will ascend above the heights of the clouds,
> I will be like the Most High' (Isa. 14:13, 14)."

Have you noticed the key word here? It's the same one Solomon used to describe his search for material possessions: the word *I*. Five times in this passage the words *I will* are used to explain Satan's haughtiness:

"I will ascend to heaven." Satan was determined to "boot" God out, remove Him as the supreme authority of the universe and replace Him with his own authority. (When we want to be independent of God, we are reflecting this same attitude.)

"I will raise my throne above the stars of God." In the Bible, the word *stars* refers to angels (Job 38:7). Satan is saying, "I am going to usurp God's authority over the angelic creation." Satan is not a small planner! In fact, he was so successful, one-third of the angelic realm bought into his coup d'état.

"I will sit on the mount of the congregation." The word *mountain* in Scripture is used for authority or rule. Satan planned to design his own kingdom and control the affairs of the universe in accordance with his own personal program. When we act independently of

God's authority over our lives, we change the Lord's Prayer into the Devil's Prayer: "Our father who is in hell, hallowed be thy name. Thy kingdom come. Thy will be done."

"I will ascend above the heights of the clouds." Clouds are used to refer to the glory of God since God often revealed His glory in the context of a cloud. When Israel was being led through the wilderness, they were led by the glory cloud. When the tabernacle was completed, Exodus 40:33 tells us that "the glory of the Lord came in the cloud." Satan wants us to show him off rather than God.

"I will be like the Most High." Satan wanted to function autonomously, no longer answering to anyone but himself. *God never answers to anyone outside Himself, Satan thought, so why should I?* He wanted to be the one who oversaw what everyone else would do.

The heart of Satan's attitude is pride. (It's ours also.) It's part of Satan's nature. (And ours too.)

Scripture gives Satan a myriad of names and descriptions to describe his nature and plans. He is called "the deceiver" (1 Tim. 4:1) because of his ability to keep men from truth as he simultaneously leads them down a road of falsehood. In fact, he is called "the father of lies" (John 8:44). He is called "the lawless one" because of his rebellion against God and his efforts to get human beings to do likewise. He is referred to as "an angel of light" (2 Cor. 11:14) because of his ability to trick men into following him rather than God.

Satan is not the dark side of an evil impersonal force as in Star Wars. Instead, he is a person who possesses intelligence, emotions, and will. His ultimate plan is to get us to act independently of God—and then lure us into his kingdom.

That's a thumbnail sketch of Satan. Now let's look at those two other enemies, who are more aligned with Satan than we would like to admit.

THE WORLD

Our word *world* comes from the Greek word *cosmos,* which was used to denote order. When the Bible talks about the cosmos, it is describing an organized diabolical hierarchy in which Satan manipulates legions of demons, vast earthly territory, and a considerable number of human beings to leave God out of the picture.

Do you remember what Satan told Jesus during His temptation in the wilderness? The Lord was shown all the kingdoms of the world in an instant. "All this authority I will give You, and their glory," the devil told Him, "for this has been delivered to me, and I give it to whomever I wish. Therefore, if You will worship before me, all will be Yours" (Luke 4:6, 7).

Most people don't spend much time picturing Satan as the owner/operator of this world order. That's because people see the things of this world (which, of themselves, are neither good nor bad), rather than the system that's *behind* those things. And that system is headed by Satan, even though he does an admirable job of painting and decorating to make it look otherwise.

Paul made it clear that Christians can enjoy the things of this cosmos (1 Tim. 6:17) as long as they maintain their dependence on and first love for God. Just as no wife can have an intimate relationship with her husband if he is having an affair with another woman, God cannot have an intimate relationship with us if we are having an affair with the world.

John told Christians they should not love the world because it is transitory. Like Disneyland or rides at the state fair, this world can produce momentary excitement, stimulation, and enjoyment. However, the thrill is short-lived.

I love amusement parks; my kids love amusement parks. But there is one reality associated with any and all amusement parks. After little more than sixty seconds it's time to exit and let someone else on the ride. So you go from ride to ride seeking new excitement by the minute, often standing in line one hour for a thrill that only lasts one minute. This is precisely what the world offers, according to John. It can give you quite a thrill; but it lasts only a moment and costs you valuable time and resources with absolutely nothing to show for your investment. Ask the guy who started experimenting with marijuana and has now graduated to crack cocaine about the loss of time and resources for a momentary thrill that leaves you with nothing in return, or the girl who has lived from one sexual encounter to another and only has loneliness, heartache, and despair to show for her efforts. It is the love of God and not the love of the world that makes living in the world worthwhile.

You and I are faced with the same choice Jesus had to make in the wilderness. Will we bow to Satan and buy into his agenda? Or will we respond, as Jesus did, "It is written: Worship the Lord your God and serve Him only" (Luke 4:8, NIV).

It really does boil down to an either/or choice. There are only two gods to choose from: the god of this world or the God of the universe. To select one is to reject the other.

So, are Christians called to closet themselves away from the trappings of the world, to shun convenience, entertainment, and technology as some sects have done?

Swinging to that extreme misses the point of Scripture. Remember, we are to be in the world, but not of the world (see John 17:15, 16).

Notice in 1 Corinthians 7:31, Paul commended those who "use the world as not misusing it. For the form of this world is passing away." Use the things of this world, he said, but don't lose sight of your first priority.

It's okay to have a television. It's okay to have a nice home. It's okay to drive a nice car. Use those things. But don't abuse them.

How do you know when you're growing too attached to your belongings? When the things you possess start possessing you.

When that new television starts competing successfully for your devotion time, God is being left out. When the new house, or the yard work, or the shopping trip, or anything else begins to rise toward first place in your life, God is being left out.

There is no hard and fast rule; we must each examine our hearts if we want to keep our relationship with the Lord vital and flourishing. For one believer, having a television anywhere in the house is a dangerous temptation. Another may have five sets and a satellite dish and still serve God faithfully. Be honest with yourself.

Here's another reliable measure of our entanglement with the things we possess. How would we feel if we lost them? A healthy Christian, like Paul, knows how to live with abundance, yet doesn't gripe or complain during the lean times.

When economic downturns sent the petroleum industry spinning some years ago, a former oil company executive I know lost his job, left his comfortable home, and moved to California to seek work. His new position paid considerably less than he was accustomed to making. For some time, he and his wife lived in a small mobile home. Granted, they were far from destitute. But throughout this experience, their faith thrived. They had learned the secret of enjoying possessions, but not clinging to them so tightly that they could not survive a loss.

We have been speaking about the battle that rages *around* us in the world. However, there's another battle raging and it's the one taking place *within* us. Our flesh is involved in a life-and-death struggle with the things of the Spirit of God. The winner controls our life—and there can be but one winner!

THE FLESH

When I refer to the flesh, I'm talking about more than the wrapping that keeps our muscles from falling off our bones. When the Bible refers to the flesh, it suggests our evil nature, those desires, patterns of thinking, behaviors, and attitudes that dwell so deeply within us. When the craving for self-satisfaction rears its head in our lives, that's the flesh. When the urge strikes to put God second and ourselves first, that's the flesh.

We're quick to shift the blame when sin catches up with us: "The Devil made me do it!" Perhaps. But it's equally likely that we sinned because we wanted to. Consciously or unconsciously, we elected to cave into our craving.

Let's be honest. The reason we're easily tempted to gratify the flesh is because it's gratifying to gratify the flesh. We feel bad afterwards but we still sin.

Just What Is Sin, Anyway?

Since none of us can escape sin, we would do well to understand exactly what it is. The Greek word for *sin* literally means to "miss the mark." It describes a bowman who drew back his string, released his arrow, but failed to hit the bull's-eye. Similarly, sin is shooting at the target and missing it. What is the target? What mark do men miss? Paul told the Roman Christians, "All have sinned and fall short of the glory of God" (Rom. 3:23). We sin when we fail to properly reflect God's glory.

To help us understand this concept, I must attack a popular myth maintained by the media, the literary community, and sometimes even the church itself. The fable is that sin can be measured by degree. For many of us, criminals seem like heavyweight sinners, while those of us who tell little white lies are light-weight sinners. It appears logical to believe that those in county jail have not sinned as seriously as those in the federal penitentiary. But sin looks quite different from God's perspective.

In the Bible sin is not measured by degree. We either fall short of God's glory or we don't. Since the entire sin question pivots on this point, let's make sure we understand God's glory.

The word *glory* means to put something on display. Sin is missing the mark, and the mark is to properly "put God on display." When we view the issue from this perspective, our understanding of sin begins to change. If we have done anything that does not accurately reveal who God is, then we have sinned.

Has it ever bothered you that God penalized Adam and Eve so severely for eating that piece of fruit? On the surface, the punishment seems disproportionate to the offense. But you see, the primary issue was not fruit. In their disobedience and rebellion, Adam and Eve deflected God's glory. To do that is sin, whether you do it a lot, or just a little. To God, sin is a yes or no issue—there are no shades of grey in between.

The story is told of two men who were exploring an island when a volcano erupted. In moments, the two found themselves surrounded by molten lava. Several feet away was a clearing—and a path to safety. To get there, however, they would have to jump across the river of melted rock.

The first man was an active senior citizen, but hardly an outstanding physical specimen. He ran as fast as he could, took an admirable leap, but traveled only a few feet. He met a swift death in the superheated lava.

The other explorer was a much younger, more virile man, in excellent physical condition. In fact, the college record he set in the broad jump remained unbroken. He put all his energy into his run, jumped with flawless form and shattered his own college record. Unfortunately, he landed six inches short of the clearing.

Though the younger man easily outperformed his companion, both found themselves equally dead. Survival was so far out of reach, ability became a non-issue.

Degrees of "goodness" may be important when hiring an employee or choosing neighbors, but when the issue is sin, the only standard that matters is God's perfect standard of holiness.

Maybe you are struggling with a piercing feeling of jealousy or inadequacy, or a burning, lustful urge. Maybe it's a temper that reaches the boiling point too often, or a constant problem with lying or gossiping. Maybe it's an addiction to drugs and/or alcohol.

Whatever you face, small or large, a habit of the flesh is out of control. It gnaws at your soul every day and seems to bombard you from all directions. Even if you face the problem squarely and vow to overcome it, the situation always ends the same way—eventually it wins out, and you are left feeling defeated, frustrated, and guilty.

The flesh has scored again.

At the risk of oversimplifying the issue, it's our job to make sure our flesh loses.

Many people would rather run than fight. In another situation, that might be an effective strategy. Unfortunately, you can't run away from your own flesh. Just because you become a Christian doesn't mean that your old man—and the desires that go with it—suddenly vanish in a puff of smoke. Nor can you put the flesh in its place simply by deciding that you want to.

In order to defeat evil, something more potent than evil must do the work. And you and I don't qualify.

The war rages on day after day. But the decisive battle has already been fought and won. The terms of surrender are spelled out in 2 Corinthians 5:17: "Therefore if anyone is in Christ, he is a new creation; old things have passed away; behold all things have become new."

New Person, Same Address

The Bible tells us—and I've mentioned it before—we are made brand new when we are saved. We are not the people we were before we accepted Jesus Christ.

The logical question is, "If I am a new person, why am I dealing with so many old problems?" Very simple. The *new you* is still living in the *old body*. Scripture tells us that we don't get new bodies until we're with Jesus. In the meantime, our spirits reside in the same "houses" we've always had—our flesh, which is thoroughly rehearsed at the art of sinning.

Many people who plead with God for deliverance from the habit of sin wake up the next day—and the day after that—facing the same old dilemmas. These disgruntled souls shake their fists and yell, "Where is God? I prayed and prayed, and I've done all the right things. I've heard all the right speakers. I've read all the right books, but my problem is still here."

The fact of the matter is, God loves us and will provide the power we need to change. But even with the King of Kings in our hearts, our hearts are temporarily residing within our unredeemed flesh. That leaves us with a weakness Satan will exploit for all it's worth. And if we give our old nature a chance, it can leap out with a sneer, take over, and trap us with the same sins we've tried so hard to overcome.

So if all of us are trapped in our flesh, how can we tell the pagans from the saints? The distinction can be found in this tongue-twister: *You may sin the same sin you used to sin when you were a sinner, but you don't sin the same sin the same way.*

Obviously, some explanation is needed. Once Christ comes into your life, He plants a new seed and you are born again. The seed sprouts and begins to grow. As soon as that occurs, you should become aware of conflict. If sin still seems as normal to you as breathing, it is doubtful that you are truly a new creature inside. You're either living a carnal life or you never really gave your life to Christ at all.

On the other hand, a healthy Christian is keenly aware of the conflict. The apostle Paul put it this way: "I know that in me (that is, in my flesh) nothing good dwells; for the will is present with me, but how to perform what is good I do not find" (Rom. 7:18).

Why is there still such a struggle between good and evil? Why do you feel like you can't stop yourself from making wrong choices?

If you are a Christian in the clutches of sin, you are not a slave, you are a *voluntary recruit*. In Christ you were given the freedom to choose. When a Christian says, "You don't understand, I just can't help myself," he is actually deceiving himself. You don't have to do anything that's related to sin with Jesus in your heart. The Lord gives you the power to turn away from sin because He gives you a brand new nature.

But you are still free to follow your own inclinations. Although Satan can't control you, he can still encourage you to go against God. He still has a toehold in your unredeemed flesh that tempts your new redeemed nature. You are caught in a war between your old flesh and the new you.

The devil has been beaten off the throne and isn't very happy living in exile. He is especially angry with those who turn their lives over to God. You are among those Satan wants, and he is extremely anxious to help you disobey.

Only by focusing on and believing what Christ has done for you will you have the confidence and backing you need to stop letting sin overwhelm you.

You Have a Friend Alongside You

The apostle Paul told the Ephesian Christians, "Be strong in the Lord and in the strength of His might" (Eph. 6:10). In our humanity, we haven't the power to overcome angels—even fallen ones like the devil and his legions. (Psalm 8 makes it clear that God created us a "little lower than the angels.") The bottom line is this: You can't beat the devil on your own.

Let me illustrate the point this way: Submarines can dive because they are pressurized. But even the most advanced submarine cannot descend below a certain level without being crushed like a soda pop can under a freight train. The pressure inside the sub must be high enough to counteract the enormous pressure of the water at such depths.

Yet, well below the maximum reach of any submarine, certain species of fish swim around happily. Why? Their internal pressure matches the external pressure. Despite their small size, they have been specially equipped to survive in the deep.

Jesus is the only one who is adequately "pressurized" to outdive the devil. He proved that when He rose from the grave. With Jesus, we can go as deep as we need to go. Without Him, we're sure to be crushed.

God Himself is the only one capable of putting the devil in his place—and that's exactly what He'll do someday. (That place is described for us in Revelation 20.) In the meantime, the Lord limits Satan's reach. In addition, He empowers us to achieve victory in our day-to-day encounters with darkness.

In Acts 19:13–17, we read about some nonbelieving Jewish exorcists who decided to try expelling demons by magically chanting the name of Jesus. "We adjure you by the Jesus whom Paul preaches," they'd say. The spirit answered them, "Jesus I know and Paul I know, but who are you?" The spirit leaped on them, thrashed them soundly, and sent them out naked and wounded.

Jesus' name is not a magic formula, though we see it used that way by some preachers and TV personalities. Paul's strength—and ours—is the product of an abiding, growing, personal intimacy with the Lord, not some high-sounding chant or incantation. Our strength is not accumulated or earned. It is supplied by the grace of God, who equips us to live the life to which He has called us.

I remember getting involved in back-alley boxing matches when I was a child. That wasn't a good thing for me because I didn't like being punched in the face. One day, I put on the gloves and prepared to fight. I stood before a pretty good-sized fellow. Though I wasn't showing it on the outside, I was petrified.

But I had a friend in my corner, sort of a mock trainer. He was pumping me with gallons of confidence: "Man, you can do it," he said. "You got a couple of inches of reach on him. I saw the way you hit the baseball yesterday! Remember how you hit it across the roof over there? Well, look, if you have that much power hitting that baseball, this guy doesn't stand a chance!"

He went on and on, pumping me up and telling me about my outstanding athletic abilities. (It's amazing what we'll believe when we're desperate!) Eventually, I squared my shoulders and stepped into the ring with a confident strut.

I began to believe what he was telling me. And as soon as I began to believe, all the nervousness evaporated. Confidence began to well up inside me. And it was all because my friend gave me a new way to add things up.

How much more confidence should we have when we have Christ to back up our calculations?

This is not to say that the day will ever come when we will awaken in the morning totally free from temptation. Even though some sects teach that perfection in this life is achievable, I don't see that doctrine in my Bible. I do read a lot there, however, to tell me how to block Satan's attack successfully.

HOW TO BLOCK SATAN'S ATTACK

The apostle Peter warned early Christians about the devil. He said, "Be sober, be vigilant; because your adversary the devil walks about like a roaring lion, seeking whom he may to devour" (1 Peter 5:8).

Think about that for a minute. When do lions roar? When they are seeking to kill their prey? No. They sneak up on them and kill them. Then, they roar. Why?

Lions are afraid of jackals, animals that travel in packs and feed off dead carcasses. Lions know that if the jackals ever show up the lions will have to flee. So the lions roar to scare off the jackals. A lion simply can't handle a pack of jackals.

So it is with Satan and his enemy, Christians. Satan roars to intimidate us, but if we would only show up and stand firm in our position, he would have to flee, instead of us. This is why James said, resist the devil and he will flee from you (4:4).

Satan is most effective when he works secretly, behind the scenes. He would prefer to let others get the credit for his work. In fact, Satan is perfectly happy if he can convince you that he does not exist at all. That's why he disguises most of his attacks so they seem to be coming from other sources—most notably, from other people. Your mate. Your children. Your coworker. Your neighbor.

Look closer and you're bound to see Satan behind the scenes, pulling the strings and pushing the buttons. He uses people to engineer our spiritual downfall by driving wedges between us that shatter our unity and draw our focus away from God.

It is a dangerous thing to take a lion for granted. Sure, he may look calm and peaceful, perhaps even soft and furry. But take my advice: Don't stick your hand near his mouth. It might not come back. However, if you look closely, you'll notice the lion is inside a cage that will protect you if you allow it to.

A boy went to the zoo with his dad. As they passed by the lion's den, one of the ferocious creatures let loose with a loud roar. Startled, the child reared back and bumped into his father. He covered his face and began to cry. The father asked, "What's wrong, Son?"

The frightened child replied, "Daddy, didn't you see the lion?"

"Yes, Son," the father said, "but I also see the cage."

Are you frightened by the lion or comforted by the cage? Jesus Christ can confine and control this adversary who has already been judged, condemned, and defeated.

What must you do? First, recognize that Satan is a defeated foe. He has no claim over you if you know Christ.

1. Recognize That Satan Is a Defeated Foe.

Calvary was the definitive blow that sealed the devil's fate. When Jesus Christ died on the cross, a cataclysmic thing happened: Satan was soundly and completely defeated. He was beaten beyond hope of recovery and he knows it!

You may ask, "If Satan is defeated, how come I have habits I can't kick? Why are there problems I can't overcome and challenges I can't face? If this guy has been so soundly defeated, why is he so powerful?"

Satan *is* defeated. But like a person beaten in life, he doesn't want to go down alone.

During a recent season, the NBA's Dallas Mavericks missed the play-offs by a country mile. Still, during their final game, they played with a passion for victory. Why? Because dealing a late-season loss to a rival team might affect that team's chances of becoming champions. In other words, "We may not be going to the play-offs, but neither are you!" In the sports world, that's the way the game is played.

Satan's goal is to rob us of our own spiritual "championship bid" and drag us down to his level. If you're saved, he can't drag you into hell, but he *can* try to render you ineffective and miserable on earth. Satan knows what Paul knew—that God has "blessed us with every spiritual blessing in the heavenly places with Christ" (Eph. 1:3). The devil understands our potential; he knows what God can make of us. And he is committed to seeing to it that we never reach that potential.

No doubt, this leads you to the next logical question: Why does God allow a defeated foe to continue waging war? The answer is fairly simple: God uses these skirmishes to reveal His glory. Every time we resist the devil, we are "strutting our stuff," as I mentioned in the last chapter. We hit the bull's-eye because we are giving glory to God.

To resist the devil, first remember that Satan is defeated. Secondly, take inventory of the armor God has provided to enable you to do battle and win.

2. Take Inventory of the Armor God Has Given You.

When our troops landed in the Middle East, they were accompanied by an enormous amount of high-tech weaponry: smart bombs that could change direction in flight and go through front doors; helicopters that could see at night; fighter bombers that could move at supersonic speed. But many of these weapons were untested. The allied forces had to ask themselves, "Will all this high-tech stuff work since a lot of the weapons have only been used in practice?"

Of particular intrigue were the heros of the war in the Gulf: patriot missiles. When Iraq launched its scud missile attacks against Israel to lure them into the conflict, these marvels of engineering would disengage the scuds "in heavenly places" before they could do much damage on the ground.

In much the same way, Christians have been equipped by God with all the necessary equipment of spiritual warfare to disengage our spiritual enemy, Satan, and render him and his cohorts ineffective in their attempts to bring us to spiritual defeat. Only by knowing, and utilizing our spiritual armament can we experience the glorious victory achieved for us at Calvary.

OUR PATRIOT MISSILES

Doing spiritual battle requires more than a New Year's resolution and a dose of willpower. Spiritual warfare requires spiritual weaponry. Paul describes these weapons to the Ephesians:

> Therefore take up the whole armor of God, that you may be able to withstand in the evil day, and having done all, to stand. Stand therefore, having girded your waist with truth, having put on the breastplate of righteousness, and having shod your feet with the preparation of the gospel of peace; above all, taking the shield of faith with which you will be able to quench all the fiery darts of the wicked one. And take the helmet of salvation, and the sword of the Spirit, which is the word of God (Eph. 6:13–17).

I can envision Paul in his prison cell, dictating this letter to the Ephesian church. Perhaps he paused, searching for a proper illustration to help him communicate this vital truth. Suddenly, his gaze fell on the Roman centurion to whom he was chained. Noticing the various components of the guard's uniform, Paul had the perfect illustration necessary to describe the vital pieces of armor considered "standard issue" in God's army.

The Belt of Truth

Roman soldiers wore a special belt around their waist. What made it unique was that other key parts of their armor connected to the belt. That way, when the soldier started running, his armor didn't shake, rattle, and roll; it was stabilized by his belt. The belt, then, was the central piece of a soldier's uniform—not an accessory as we sometimes view it today.

The application for us is clear. None of the rest of our armor will hold together if we do not begin with a commitment to the truth. In some circles of our society, truth has undergone a change in meaning. In most school systems, for example, truth is a relative concept. There's *my* truth and *your* truth, and they don't have to be the same truth. Biblical truth, however, is objective truth, based on the absolute authority of a perfect, holy God. Biblical truth is not a matter of what you like or how you feel. We talked about the necessity of the Bible in chapter six, so let me just add that God's Word is the belt that supports all the rest of our spiritual lives. This objective standard will keep our spiritual clothes from blowing uncontrollably in the changing wind of secularism, emotionalism, or relativism.

The Breastplate of Righteousness

Hooked into the Roman soldier's belt was a breastplate, which covered his most vital organ: his heart. After all, an arrow or sword in the heart meant instant death.

When Paul told us to wear the breastplate of righteousness, he was saying, "Cover your heart." Of course, in this context, the heart connotes much more than a blood-pumping muscle. It represents the core of our inner being.

The Christian heart is Satan's prime target, for there resides the conscience, our internal standard of right and wrong. And Satan has been all too successful in blurring the dividing line between right and wrong in our society. That's how homosexuality becomes an "alternative lifestyle," how raw greed turns into "upward mobility," and how obscenity passes off as "free-

232 – THE VICTORIOUS CHRISTIAN LIFE

dom of expression." Sin is easily rationalized in the absence of conscience.

Our conscience is not easily neutralized. That's why the first time we do something wrong, we feel extremely uncomfortable. Succeeding offenses, however, become less troublesome until, at last, a new habit is formed.

It reminds me of the story of a young boy who went fishing one day. While hunting for bait, he happened upon a nest of small, red worms. He picked one up, and as he placed it on the hook, the worm bit him. It hurt a lot, but the boy shrugged off the pain and dropped the line in the water. A moment later, he caught a good-sized catfish. Thinking that he had happened upon a tasty new bait, he reached for another worm. Again, he was bitten, but the pain was less intense. He baited his hook, dropped it in the water, and pulled out another fish in a matter of moments. No doubt about it—the fish couldn't get enough of those worms.

Sometime later, the boy hiked back to the road with a stringer full of fish. A passing motorist saw the boy's catch and stopped to offer him a ride. "How'd you catch so many fish, Son?" the man asked.

"I found these red worms. They bite, but you get used to it."

The man looked at the boy's hand and knew at once what had happened. He rushed the boy to the hospital, but it was too late. The child died on the way.

You see, those worms were really baby rattlesnakes. Each successive bite, though less painful, added more venom to his system, until the boy was overcome.

If Satan can neutralize our conscience, we become easy prey for his venom.

So how do we keep a pure heart? By keeping our heart sheltered behind the breastplate of righteousness, hooked securely to that belt of truth.

If my heart tells me to do something that contradicts God's truth, I know that I have a "heart disorder." Remember, only God's truth is absolute; our innermost thoughts and emotions must be brought into line with the Word.

Peace Shoes

No soldier can fight without a sure footing. Proper shoes enable him to move forward in battle.

The Christian can only move forward in his spiritual walk if he stands firmly on the foundation of peace. When Paul talked about the "gospel of peace," he inferred two specific kinds of peace: peace *with* God and the peace *of* God.

Peace with God is what we call "positional" peace, which can be compared to signing a treaty to end a war. Though the treaty signals the end of the fighting, it does not necessarily end the conflict that caused it. In the same way, having peace with God means that, by His grace, we have come into a right relationship with Him. Our personal war against the kingdom of God has ended. Even so, we may still experience the turmoil and inner conflict that characterized our old life.

On the other hand, the peace *of* God is that inner tranquility and sense of well-being that transcends our circumstances. That's why Paul called it the peace that "passes understanding." We talked about that kind of peace and joy in the last chapter so let me just remind you: Christians need to live in light of their salvation, not in light of their circumstances.

The Shield of Faith

First, notice that the shield of faith is the only piece of armor that is mobile. You can move it around as needed. If your breastplate is hanging loose on one side, you can cover the exposed area with your shield. If you left your belt unbuckled, slide the shield in front of it. There's only one part of your body a shield won't protect: your back. The last thing you do during a battle is show the enemy your back.

We must face our enemy head-on. As we do, we can depend on the shield of faith to cover any weaknesses that may remain in the rest of our armor. New Christians who have yet to develop a mature Christian lifestyle should be encouraged by the fact they have a shield to protect them while they cinch up the loose pieces of armor in their lives.

Whatever we lack can be "made up" by faith, which is defined as "the substance of things hoped for, the evidence of things not seen" (Heb. 11:1). Wherever we are deficient, we can depend on God to make up the difference—even if that help doesn't seem apparent. After all, faith is the evidence of things *not seen*. This armor of faith is designed to deflect "fiery darts" or arrows. Anyone who's ever seen a western movie knows about flaming arrows. Unlike the ordinary arrows the Indians used, these were not aimed at people. Buildings, wagons, haystacks, and the like were their targets. The intent was to start fires. The strategy made sense: If the enemy could keep you busy dealing with the fire, you'd be less able to defend yourself. The Indians knew that the cowboys couldn't fight fire and Indians at the same time.

In the same way, Satan bombards us with a barrage of flaming arrows designed to draw our attention away from his frontal assault. One arrow may be aimed at your marriage in the hopes of kindling some tension between you and your spouse. Another takes dead aim at your kids. Your health may be a target as well. Still other arrows land in your workplace, among your circle of friends, or even in your church.

If we become consumed with putting out fires, we become easy targets for attack.

Ah, but don't forget your shield of faith. It's dependable and mobile. You can easily maneuver it to stand firmly between you and the oncoming volley of arrows.

Your faith will protect you, provided it is the right kind of faith. You could have enormous faith in gifted preachers, talented choirs, or your most zealous Christian friends. But that kind of faith won't get you anywhere. *The intensity of your faith is irrelevant if the object of your faith is erroneous.*

On the other hand, if your faith is centered squarely on Jesus Christ, a little bit of faith is all you need. If my faith is genuine, even though Satan may set my world on fire, I will continue to focus on the supernatural enabling Jesus Christ has provided to me. That kind of confidence is like water to a fire. God throws open the hydrant of His grace!

There is only one way to know if you are using your shield of faith. Ask yourself, "Am I being obedient to God and His Word." The proof of faith is that you are doing what God says to do because you believe He is going to honor your obedience, even though you don't know how, when, or where.

I discovered the meaning of the shield of faith during my seminary days. One of the ways I worked my way through seminary was by loading and unloading buses at the Trailways bus station in Dallas. I worked the 11:00 P.M. to 7:00 A.M. schedule, fondly called the "deadman's shift." This was back-breaking work, often done in extremes of bitter cold or blazing heat.

My coworkers had devised a number of deceptive schemes to get out of work, like clocking each other in from their next break when in reality they were sleeping, going to all-night bookstores, or even going back home. I would not participate in these deceptions, so fiery darts came to me from every direction. My coworkers left the heavier bags for me to unload; they called me, "Rev.," "Preacher," and "the fanatic." Some disliked me simply because I was an ever-present reminder of their sin. Yet I stood my ground. I promised God I would honor His standards and do the best job I could, as long as I was there.

Some weeks later I received a call to come to the head manager's office. He told me that unknown to any of us on the nightshift, the company management had been sending spies to check on us, dressed like bus passengers so we would never suspect them. They had brought back the report that I was faithful to my responsibilities while many of the other guys were fooling around. "Even though you are a newer employee, we want you to be the new night supervisor."

The lesson I learned that night, I have never forgotten. When you keep Satan from distracting you, you put out his fiery darts. So it is with every believer. Faith that obeys God blocks Satan's attempts to distract us from the road to spiritual victory.

The Helmet of Salvation

The need for a helmet is obvious. You can survive the loss of limbs; certain organs can be repaired or replaced. But no one has survived the loss of the brain.

Without the brain, you can't move, you can't think, you can't speak, you can't react.

Your brain controls your body; it calls the shots. In the same way, your mind (your conscious thoughts and attitudes) drives your spirit. Is it any wonder that Satan wants access to our minds?

Salvation in the Bible is spoken of in three tenses: *salvation past* from the penalty of sin, *salvation present* from the power of sin, and *salvation future* from the very presence of sin. Since Paul's concern here was spiritual warfare, he wished that Christians no longer operated under sin's power and that demanded a new way of thinking.

Until Christians change the way they think, they can't change the way they live, for "as [a man] thinks in his heart, so is he" (Prov. 23:7).

This renewal of the mind does not happen by osmosis. It is a planned change that occurs because we expose ourselves to God's truth and allow that truth to govern our attitudes and actions. Paul expressed the power of having a biblical mind-set when he told the Christians at Philippi that he had learned the secret of victorious Christian living. He wrote, "I can do all things through Christ who strengthens me" (Phil. 4:13). Rather than thinking in terms of a defeated, powerless Christian, he viewed himself as a super, victorious saint. He saw himself from the standpoint of who he was in Christ rather than who he used to be outside of Christ. Until Christians think in terms of their new identity instead of their old one, they can never be victorious. All Satan has to do is give them a mental relapse into their pre-Christ mind-set.

PUTTING ON THE ARMOR

God has told us that in order to defeat Satan, we must put on the *whole* armor. A single belt or a lone breastplate won't do the job.

How do I actually go about putting on all of these spiritual resources? You can't just waltz into K-Mart and pick up a helmet of salvation!

Spiritual resources are appropriated by prayer. Paul told the Exphesians, "With all prayer and petition, pray at all times in the Spirit, and with this in view, be on the alert with all perseverance and petition for all the saints" (Eph. 6:18, NIV).

Have you ever had one of those nightmares where you drive to work, greet everybody on the job, pour a cup of coffee, and suddenly realize you forgot your purse or wallet? Embarrassing, isn't it? Well, that nightmare comes true every day for people who try to live the Christian life with nothing more than their human resources. Without prayer, you are a spiritual pauper.

There are many naked warriors in God's army who think they're well-dressed. If your prayer life is anemic, I suggest you check your armor before testing it in battle.

If Jesus, who knew He was God, knew that He could not function without prayer, how much more should we mortals long to spend time on our knees?

God has equipped us with spiritual patriot missiles—the armor of God. He has promised us that these weapons will work in battle. They have, in fact, been tested by Christians for a couple thousand years by that cloud of witnesses I mentioned in the last chapter. Let's use these spiritual weapons to disengage Satan's weapons "in heavenly places" before they do much damage in our lives. The battle is won. We just have to join the ranks!

12

THE OVERCOMERS

I SUSPECT THAT if the apostle Paul were alive today, he might be the type of man who would think, *The news and editorial sections of the paper are there only to keep the rain off the sports section.* He used athletic analogies in many of his letters, particularly the analogy of the Christian life as a race.

The Hebrew Christians were considering giving up because they were being persecuted by their fellow Jews. Paul urged them to "run with endurance the race that is set before us" (Heb. 12:1).

Most of us believe Paul's analogy. We agree that the Christian life is a race—and not just an ordinary race, but a marathon. A 26-mile marathon requires not only that we run, but that we run with endurance.

Anyone can run a 100-yard dash. Even a 300-pound couch potato can slog his out-of-shape carcass 300 feet down a track. Obviously, he won't set any records—at least, not for speed. But, most likely, he will eventually cross the line.

A marathon is another story. The victorious Christian life is a marathon. And that marathon is a lot like the road to the Superbowl. There are many bumps, bruises, disappointments, and challenges along the way. However, the pains of the struggle seem more than worth it when it is time to receive the prize.

One day God is going to hand out rewards to His overcomers—those Christians who weathered the storms of life and crossed the finish line victorious. Their desire, discipline, and determination will be applauded by the Lord and the heavenly host on that final day of reckoning.

Will you be an overcomer? Will I?

In one sense all Christians are overcomers. John wrote, "For whatever is born of God overcomes the world. And this is the victory that has overcome the world—our faith. Who is he who overcomes the world, but he who believes that Jesus is the Son of God" (1 John 5:4, 5). In other words, believers are overcomers because "greater is He who is in us than he who is in the world." By virtue of our position in Christ we are already overcomers.

Sadly, though, not all overcomers *overcome.* All Christians have made the cut and are on God's team. We all have the same coach, we all wear the same spiritual uniform, we all have access to the same biblical rules. Yet some of us won't experience the thrill of spiritual victory. Just as some pro players win a spot on the team, yet never win a championship, some Christians will end life as failures rather than victors. When the final gun sounds to end the game of our lives, a few of us will say to the Lord, "I couldn't make it. I just couldn't make it."

And God, like a stern coach, will respond, "Yes, you could. I already made you an overcomer. You just refused to overcome." Make no mistake about it, God wants you to be an overcomer. You have joined God's team by accepting the priceless contract that Jesus Christ signed, sealed, and delivered at Calvary. That required no work and no talent on your part.

But while salvation is free, sanctification is expensive. We have to be willing to pay the price to win the prize, and to do that, we have to stay in the race to reach the finish line. Someday we all will look into the eyes of our Judge.

THE EYES OF THE ALMIGHTY JUDGE

My father was a longshoreman who worked on the waterfront in Baltimore, loading and unloading ships. Each day he called in to check his orders to see if he should report to work that day and, if so, at what time; it just depended on what ship was in and how much cargo had to be unloaded. Some days there was only enough work for one hour; other days he could work around the clock. We never knew when he was coming home.

On one occasion my father left me instructions to do some work for him around the house while he was gone. Unfortunately, this was in the summertime, and my joy and passion was to play baseball, not get my work done. So I decided to play the end against the middle. Since I didn't know when Dad was returning—there was no way to find out—I averaged how much he had worked previously that week and divided it in half. I reasoned that as long as I returned home before that amount of time had passed I'd be OK.

Wouldn't you know it? They only needed him for a few hours. He returned home and tracked me down in the back alley, where I was busy hitting home runs. He yelled, "Tony, come here. NOW!" He had returned unexpectedly and caught me in defeat. I got the spanking of my life.

Similarly, many Christians are playing spiritual roulette with the return of Christ. "It's far off," they say, "and I won't be dying soon, so I have a long time to develop a consistently victorious Christian life."

Early Christians used the same rationalizations. So the apostle John wrote the seven churches of Asia Minor to let them know that they were hedging their bets. Jesus Christ, the Judge, is judging His people *now*, he said, to determine how He will reward them later. So you'd better shape up before it's too late!

The judge painted in Revelation 1 is certainly not the meek and mild, Downey-soft Jesus we are accustomed to. Neither is it a "shuckin, jivin" Jesus, like the one protrayed in "Jesus Christ, Superstar." This Jesus is a Judge, with eyes of fire, feet like bronze, and an authoritative voice like the sound of many waters. He sits in the midst of His people to render a verdict on their commitment to Him as their Lord (vv. 13–16).

Just as you can never expect to be victorious in sports by taking the game lightly, Christians cannot expect to be overcomers if we take our faith and our Lord lightly. John reminded the Christians of Asia Minor about key principles that would help them to finish the race victoriously—and then he told them the reward that will follow.

His message to the seven churches and to us is crystal clear: "Christians who are overcomers in God's kingdom now will receive special blessings in God's kingdom later."

Let's look at John's message to each of these churches. First the principle, then the reward. Those rewards are worthy of our exhausting lifelong marathon.

1. "Stay Devoted to Christ—and You Will Enjoy a Special Intimacy with the Lord in the Next Life."

The church at Ephesus was loveless. They had doctrine. They had duty. But they had no devotion. They had lost their passion for Jesus Christ, though they still went through the motions. They were Bible-toting, Bible-quoting Christians who wouldn't dare associate with the unorthodox. But they had no love and no intimacy for God: "I have this against you, that you have left your first love" (Rev. 2:4).

God never meant for our duty for Him to replace our love for Him. Duty and devotion must always work side by side. In fact, verse 5 says fix your church or yourself by going back to the devotion that you once exhibited. Then it says repent. In other words, change your mind. Stop being satisfied with the status quo.

When I'm in a marriage counseling session, I tell couples, "Turn back the hands of time. Do the things you used to do." People cannot have the relationship they used to have, if they aren't willing to do the things they used to do. The same is true for Christians. Intimacy with God is the result of developing a relationship. Go back to those days when you first gave control of your life to God—and do the things you used to do.

Then John gave the payoff: Those who are devoted to Christ will be given a special privilege. Verse 7 says,

"To him who overcomes, I will give to eat from the tree of life, which is in the midst of the Paradise of God."

This reminds me of when Chuck Swindoll, one of my favorite preachers, came to speak at a banquet at Dallas Theological Seminary, where I was a student. Before that day, I called his secretary, Helen, and said, "I sure would like to meet Dr. Swindoll when he comes."

She said nicely, "You know that really isn't possible." The seminary had planned to seat four thousand people, but eight thousand came. So they added another banquet room. Some still couldn't attend. Others just got to sit at the back, and didn't get to eat.

On the day before the banquet, while I was at work, my secretary said to me, "There is a Dr. Swindoll on the phone for you. Are you available?"

"Available? Give me that phone," I said.

"Evans, I heard you wanted to get with me. I've heard your sermons and I would like to meet you too. I tell you what. Before the banquet, let's meet across the street from the seminary in that little restaurant, and we'll get a table in the corner and just have some fellowship. Can you make it?"

I said, "Let me check my calendar here. Yeah, yeah. I can make it!" Consequently, I had a time of fellowship with a mentor. In the Kingdom, the saints who overcome on earth will get to go into the Paradise of God for special fellowship with Him.

2. "Don't Compromise Your Beliefs, and You Will Enjoy a Special Honor at His Wedding Feast."

The church at Pergamum was a compromising church. Balaam and Balak worked together to get Israel to intermarry with pagans. John wrote Jesus' words: "But I have a few things against you, because you have there those who hold the doctrine of Balaam, who taught Balak to put a stumbling block before the children of Israel, to eat things sacrificed to idols, and to commit sexual immorality."

While Christians can compromise on preferences, they cannot compromise on principles. We can't be one way on Sunday and another on Monday. This is a major problem among Christians in America today. We don't take a stand. We don't keep our standards. We merely adjust to satisfy society.

But consider what an overcomer receives in verse 17: "To him who overcomes I will give some of the hidden manna to eat. And I will give him a white stone, and on the stone a new name written which no one knows except him who receives it."

I've mentioned that manna was like corn flakes from heaven. Israel took some of the manna, put it in a jar, then put the jar inside the Holy of Holies in the Ark of the Covenant to remind them that God had supplied their needs in the wilderness.

No one knows the site of God's hidden supply of this special feast. But it's only for overcomers, who also will receive a white stone, which was like a theater ticket in Jesus' day, providing entrance into events and shows— a season pass, if you please.

There'll be plenty of people in heaven, but as an overcomer, you'll enjoy a special honor at the wedding feast of Christ.

3. "Remain Holy—and You Will Enjoy a Special Position of Authority under Christ."

Thyatira was an unholy church. A woman called Jezebel (either her real or a symbolic name) ran the church there. Meanwhile, she was leading many into sin. No one had confronted her. In other words, they tolerated sin. So God says in verse 22: "Indeed I will cast her into a sickbed, and those who commit adultery with her into great tribulation, unless they repent of her deeds."

This principle is reflected in 1 Corinthians 11. If you don't judge yourself, God does it for you. But the overcomer, according to Revelation 1:26–28, "keeps My works until the end, to him I will give power over the nations—He shall rule them with a rod of iron; 'They shall be dashed to pieces like the potter's vessels' —as I also have received authority from My Father; and I will give him the morning star."

This passage refers to the Millennial kingdom, which will last one thousand years. It will be run like our world today, with prime ministers, governors, and mayors, who will rule for and with Christ. Where you sit then depends on how you live now. You may not be in a position of power now, but if you serve the Lord faithfully, God will give you a position of power and prestige in His Kingdom.

When I was the Dallas Cowboys chaplain, I some- times attended practice before the Bible study. One day, I played wide receiver. Roger Staubach called a fly pattern. So I did a little "Baltimore juke," flew down the field and—bull's-eye!—I caught the football over a defender. Just after that, I heard a guest who was standing beside Coach Tom Landry say, "Oh man! Who's that? He's good!"

I didn't tell them I wasn't on the team, but they associated me with the Cowboys. One of the guests even wanted my autograph! Overcomers will get that kind of recognition in the kingdom. Our recognition will come because of our association with the morning star, which is a description the apostle Peter used for Jesus Himself (2 Peter 1:16–19). People will seek us out because of all the attention Christ gives us.

4. "Persevere—and You Will Enjoy Special Public Recognition."

The church at Philadelphia persevered through trial and tribulation and would be rewarded handsomely for their continued obedience. Overcomers who hang tough, this Scripture says, "will be made pillars in the temple" (Rev. 3:12).

When we speak of people being pillars, we are referring to their significance to a program or project. Believers who persevere are viewed by God as pillars of His Kingdom program. You don't get your name in the ring of honor at Texas Stadium because you have a great game; you have to have a great career. When Roger Staubach led the Dallas Cowboys to a Superbowl victory, the whole team received paychecks and rings, but because Staubach was consistently great throughout his career, his name is in the ring of honor.

So it is with God's most valuable saints. "He who overcomes, I will make him a pillar in the temple of My God, and he shall go out no more. I will write on him the name of My God and the name of the city of My God, the new Jerusalem, which comes down out of heaven from My God. And I will write on him My new name" (Rev. 3:12). When we stand before Jesus, if we were faithful in suffering, didn't compromise but stood fast, He will make us a part of His ring of honor. And everyone in heaven will forever know who we are.

5. "Remain Truly Committed and You Will Enjoy Special Authority."

Laodicea was located where Hierapolis and Colosse merged; Hierapolis had hot springs, Colosse cold springs. When the two merged at Laodicea, the springs, like the church, were lukewarm. "I know your works, that you are neither hot nor cold. I could wish you were cold or hot" (Rev. 3:15).

Consequently, verse 16 says, "I will spew you out of My mouth." (I'm sure God is just as eager to "excommunicate" many churches today because they are lukewarm.)

God suggests an antidote. "I counsel you to buy from Me gold refined by fire" (v. 18). In other words, be concerned about God's value system and not the secular system.

Finally He tells them, "I stand at the door and knock" (v. 20). God's talking to each of us. He's knocking on our hearts to enter into intimate fellowship with us. To those who are for Him, He says, "I will grant to him to sit down with Me on My throne, as I also overcame and sat down with My Father on His throne."

During a visit to Universal Studios in California, my family and I watched the dog for *Little House on the Prairie* perform tricks. When a gentleman announced that he needed a volunteer from the audience, my oldest son, Anthony, ran up front, put his hand in the man's face, and shouted, "Choose me!"

They did.

As my son walked around, the dog walked through his legs. When my son held something up, the dog jumped up and took it. The dog did many other tricks and the people applauded him, not my son. But because my son was part of the tricks, my son shared in the dog's glory.

In the kingdom, if you are an overcomer, God will call you forth publicly and will allow you to share in His glory.

These blessings are for each of us if we just run the race successfully. But many of us think, "It's hard having to wait until eternity to get any credit."

Henry Morrison, a great missionary to Africa, was returning home from the field on a large ship. As his boat docked in New York thousands greeted Theodore Roosevelt, who was also on the vessel. Henry Morrison had served the Lord for forty years in Africa. Yet no one was there to greet him. It broke his heart. Dejected, he walked down the plank.

Then all of a sudden it dawned on him. "Henry," a voice was saying, "don't worry. You're not home yet." Then he saw a vision in which thousands and thousands of Africans were standing at the Pearly Gates, applauding him as Peter welcomed him to glory.

So if people are not recognizing you now, if you're not getting your due, don't worry; you are not home yet. Just keep overcoming. Soon, the thrill of victory will be yours.

A STANDING OVATION?

A brilliant young pianist was giving his very first concert. As the final chord of his brilliant performance reverberated in the hall, the audience rose to its feet and broke out in thunderous applause. Only one member of the audience remained seated, clapping politely, but without particular enthusiasm.

Tears welled up in the young pianist's eyes. His head drooped slightly as he left the stage in utter defeat.

The stage manager in the great hall was a sensitive and observant man who had noticed the lone gentleman and saw how this cool response affected the star performer.

"Son," he said, "you're a hit! Everyone was overwhelmed. The critic from the *Times* was in tears. By morning, you'll be famous. Don't let one guy get you down."

"You don't understand," the dejected young man replied. "That man was my piano teacher. It only matters what he thinks."

The church has too many crowd-pleasers already. We have more than enough people who can bring television and radio audiences, congregations, and class members to their feet. What we need is a bumper crop of mature believers who are content to play to an audience of one.

That's what Stephen did. The crowd did anything but applaud as he turned his trial into an opportunity to boldly proclaim the Gospel. As he was being stoned to death, he cried out, "Lord, do not charge them with this sin" (Acts 7:60).

Jesus stood up.

It doesn't matter if the brothers and sisters in your congregation marvel at your maturity. It doesn't matter if the leaders of your church can't wait to dub you a deacon. It doesn't matter if you witness like a winner or teach like a trooper. Only one thing matters: Does Jesus stand up? Only He knows whether you're performing like a virtuoso or clowning around with the chords. Only He can tell whether the music is flowing from your heart or being played by rote from a collection of notes scrawled on a score. And only He can blend the melody from your instrument with the music of other believers to make a symphony of service that can breathe new life into your soul, your church, and your community.

I applaud the desire to grow and become a victorious Christian that led you to read this book. Your brothers and sisters in Christ will applaud your efforts to implement the principles you've learned. But don't let that applause divert your gaze from that center seat in the front row.

Continue the concert of growth, knowing that the performance is in His honor. And it should be. He wrote the song. And He will be with you until you reach the finish line.

MAKING IT TO THE FINISH LINE

A British runner named Derek Redmon competed in the 1992 Olympics. Midway through his race, he tore a ligament—a very painful injury that sent him to the ground. The rest of the pack ran on to finish the race, but poor Derek just lay there. His dreams, his hopes, and years of training collapsed along with him.

Then, something happened that drew the attention of the crowd and the television cameras away from the winner. Derek pushed himself up off the ground, stood up on wobbly legs, and began making his way around the track. He was going to finish that race.

After only a few painful strides, it was clear that running was definitely out of the question. He slowed to a walk—a slow, agonizing, tentative walk. Then a man appeared on the track. Security guards tried to deter him, but he was not to be stopped. He put his arm around Derek's shoulder and started helping him make his way toward the finish line. The TV commentators confirmed my suspicions quickly: It was Derek's father. Eventually, father and son crossed the line while the applause thundered throughout the stadium.

In the Christian race, it's not all that important who crosses the finish line first. What matters is that we stay the course. Each of us stumbles from time to time. Sometimes it seems impossible to go on.

That's when our Heavenly Father steps out of the stands. Satan may come along and claim that it is unfair for God to step out on the field. But our omnipotent Lord will not be stopped. He will enfold us in His loving arms and say, "This is my child. We're going to finish this race together."